Unveiling the Mysteries: An Introductory Archaeology Guide

Eman .X Vickers

Funny helpful tips:

Life's journey is a tapestry; weave it with threads of love, joy, and purpose.

Stay optimistic; a positive outlook can change the trajectory of challenges.

Unveiling the Mysteries: An Introductory Archaeology Guide : Journey into the Ancient Past: A Comprehensive and Engaging Introduction to Archaeology

Life advices:

In the realm of possibilities, dream big, but act with intention and purpose.

Learn to apologize sincerely; taking responsibility strengthens trust.

Introduction

This is a comprehensive guide that explores the fascinating world of archaeology, making it accessible to individuals who are new to the field. This guide covers a wide range of topics related to archaeology, providing readers with a solid foundation in this discipline.

The guide begins by defining archaeology and introducing readers to its basics. It highlights the two main branches of archaeology: research archaeology and rescue archaeology, explaining their distinct purposes and methodologies.

Readers are taken on a historical journey through the development of archaeology, gaining insight into its evolution as a scientific discipline. The guide also explores various types of archaeology, shedding light on specialized areas within the field.

Historic preservation and public archaeology are discussed, emphasizing the importance of preserving our cultural heritage and involving the public in archaeological endeavors. Ethical considerations, laws, and health and safety practices in archaeology are also covered, ensuring that readers understand the responsibilities and ethical standards of archaeologists.

The guide introduces readers to the tools and equipment commonly used in archaeological research, including ground-penetrating radar (GPR) and magnetometers. It details excavation supplies and techniques, preparing readers for the practical aspects of fieldwork.

A section on non-invasive archaeology highlights methods that minimize disturbance to archaeological sites, while excavation strategies provide insights into how archaeologists carefully uncover and document artifacts and features.

Processing finds in a laboratory is a critical aspect of archaeology, and the guide walks readers through the steps involved in handling and conserving artifacts and samples. It covers everything from washing and cataloging finds to artifact classification and analysis.

The guide emphasizes the importance of interpreting archaeological finds to reconstruct the human past. It discusses the study of settlement systems, social systems, and daily life, demonstrating how archaeologists piece together the puzzle of history.

Archaeological reports play a vital role in disseminating research findings, and the guide offers guidance on preparing these reports effectively.

This book encourages readers to think ahead and consider the significance of their contributions to the field. It empowers individuals with the knowledge and understanding needed to embark on a journey into the world of archaeology and make meaningful contributions to the study of our shared history.

Contents

What is Archaeology?

To use its simplest definition, *archaeology* is the study of human activity through the recovery and analysis of material evidence.[1]

The roots of modern archaeology venture back to antiquarianism in 19th century Europe, and its practices have evolved dramatically since then. Often classified as a social science, it is sometimes regarded as a field in its own right (or, in the case of North America, as a sub-field of anthropology).[2][3]

Just like in major motion pictures such as *Indiana Jones*, *The Mummy* and *National Treasure*, archaeology is full of excitement and discovery, but it also falls victim to a whole host of major misunderstandings. Some people believe archaeology is a romantic and adventuristic occupation, confined to the study of bejewelled artefacts and ancient ruins, but it is much broader than that. Archaeology is a *scientific* profession that involves long, painstaking and often repetitive work, carrying out surveys, excavations and processing data. It is concerned with *any* place humans have been and *any* remains they leave behind at *any* point in time – ranging from the ancient past to yesterday, and the moon to your own back garden.[4]

Another common misconception is that archaeological work is confined to a handful of professionals. The chances are that everyone does some archaeology in their daily lives without realising it. For example, you might be able to tell from the car on the driveway who is home, or from dirty dishes in the sink what someone has had for tea.

Evidence used by archaeologists can range from tiny, microscopic things such as pollen samples and DNA, to seemingly unremarkable observations such as layers and dark stains in the soil, to more glamorous finds such as beautiful brooches and majestic pyramids.

Archaeologists, therefore, are concerned with human history in its entirety – from the development of the first stone tools at Lomekwi in East Africa 3.3 million years ago until the present day. It plays a particularly important role in the studying of pre-historic societies, which lack written records for scholars to study and – most importantly of all – accounts for some 99% of human existence.[5]

Many key developments in the history of humanity occurred during prehistoric times, highlighted by the Palaeolithic period when the hominins developed from the australopithecines in Africa and eventually evolved into modern *Homo sapiens*.

On a cultural level, archaeology can also shed light on technological advances during this period, including the development of stone tools, the mastering of fire, and the origins of agriculture and religion.

Historical archaeology, meanwhile, can be used to study historic and literate cultures. Archaeological evidence remains critical in literate civilisations such as Ancient Greece because much of the surviving written evidence is incomplete or bias. In many societies, for example, literacy was restricted to a select few – i.e. priests and aristocrats – whose views and interests often differed dramatically from those of the mainstream population.

As well as involving the usual suspects – surveying, excavation and data analysis – archaeological work involves cross-disciplinary research, including the input of anthropology, history, classics, ethnology, geography, geology, linguistics, semiology, sociology, textual criticism, physics, information sciences, chemistry, statistics, paleoecology, palaeography, palaeontology, paleozoology and paleobotany.

Turn over to the next chapter to find out more about what it takes to be an archaeologist.

Archaeology: The Basics

The goals of archaeology vary, ranging from reconstructing past ways of life to explaining changes in human societies over time.

There is, however, one thing that all archaeologists share. If you're looking for money, you're in the wrong profession. Archaeologists are not treasure hunters (known in the profession as *looters*). Rather than asking how much an artefact is worth, they seek to enrich their *curiosity* by finding out how old it is, why it's there, and what you can learn about the maker or owner. Instead of keeping finds for themselves, they are typically donated to museum collections for the public to enjoy and experts to study. The goals of archaeology include:

- Studying the human past.
- Reconstructing past human behaviour and ways of life.
- Understanding past cultures (social, political, economic and religious) and how they changed over time.
- Conserving and interpreting the material record of past peoples.
- Uncovering the story of past peoples to benefit the public through enjoyment, education and practical uses.

In some ways, archaeology closely resembles detective work, and many of its methods are shared by police investigators. Some examples are:

- Recording and photographing evidence at the scene.
- Using accurate techniques to recover, process and analyse evidence.
- Conducting research to obtain background information about the people, places and times of concern.
- Interviewing people with desirable information.

- Using techniques from other scientific disciplines to obtain information from the evidence.
- Stating and arguing your interpretation of the evidence, often backed up by other experts.

Today, archaeology can be broken down into a large number of sub-disciplines, such as maritime archaeology, Marxist archaeology and archaeoastronomy. Yet as its popularity has grown, so has its problems: ranging from the looting of archaeological sites, to pseudoarchaeology, to fierce opposition to the excavation of human remains.

Archaeological work can also be frustrating due to its tediousness and the incompleteness of the archaeological record. Typically only durable materials survive, such as stone or pottery, unless specific conditions prevail that preserve organic materials (including permafrost and extreme aridity). As a result, archaeologists have – and continue to – find ingenious ways of extracting information from the remains that are available for us to study. Readily borrowing ideas from other academic disciplines, they have also adopted scientific and medical technologies (including carbon-14 dating, CAT scanning or DNA analysis) as a means of dating artefacts and tracing the genetic origins of people.

Research and Rescue Archaeology

In this book you will discover that archaeological work involves many stages – from gathering data and field surveys, to deciding whether to dig or not to dig, to analysing finds and reporting your results. There are two principal forms of fieldwork in archaeology, *research archaeology* (where the aim is to find answers to specific questions) and *rescue archaeology* (where a record is made of archaeological remains threatened by development).

Research Archaeology

One of the big benefits of research archaeology is that the archaeologist can choose what sites and subjects they want to investigate, as well as deciding what questions they want to find answers for. Such questions might be simple (i.e. 'What can I find out about past peoples who lived on this site?') or complex (i.e. 'What do features in the site's landscape reveal about religious practices and beliefs of the site's previous occupants?').

The area of research can be confined to a very compact site (e.g. a house) or cover a very large site (e.g. an entire landscape that extends hundreds of miles). The aim, on the other hand, can be very specific (e.g. to study cave paintings) or very broad and complex (e.g. examining trends in diet, religion, culture, industry or trade).

Rescue Archaeology

Rescue archaeology is centred on salvaging archaeological evidence and information before it is destroyed by development. In most countries planning legislation requires developers to consult with experts to determine the likely impact their work will have on both the natural (e.g. delicate ecosystems) and historic environment (e.g. historic buildings and buried remains).

The role of a rescue archaeologist, then, is to work (normally to a tight deadline) to make an objective assessment of the importance of the archaeological remains and decide what can be sacrificed and what needs to be excavated in order to 'rescue' important material. In some cases, the archaeological material uncovered is so important that a planned development may be altered or moved to a different location to protect the remains.

Unlike research archaeologists, rescue archaeologists do not have the luxury of choosing the site, area of study or research questions.

Archaeology versus History

People often incorrectly view historians and archaeologists as being one and the same. It is true that both history and archaeology study the human past, but other than this the two disciplines differ greatly from each other. Historians use *written* and *oral* records to study the past, which limits their areas of study to more recent, literate societies. Archaeologists, meanwhile, can venture much further back in time as well as supplementing history by searching for material evidence that does not appear in the historical record.

Archaeology versus Palaeontology

People often mistakenly think that anything that's old falls under the domain of archaeology. But that's not the case. Archaeology is only concerned with the study of *human behaviour*, using material evidence left behind by *people*.

Palaeontology, on the other hand, is the study of prehistoric species – mostly ones that are extinct and with an emphasis on fossil data.

Archaeologists only study the fossilised remains of non-human species when they can be directly associated with human activity. For example:

- Bones of animals hunted or scavenged by early humans. Given that dinosaurs died some 65 million years ago and early humans only came into being some 4 million years ago, dinosaurs are of no interest to archaeologists. Sorry Fred Flintstone!
- Fossilised remains found by humans long after the animal had died, and turned into artefacts (e.g. sharpened to make tools).

Pseudoarchaeology

Pseudoarchaeology refers to any activities that claim to be archaeological, but in reality violate established archaeological practices. This can include both fictional archaeological work (such as Hollywood blockbuster movies) and actual activity.

A classic example of a writer of pseudoarchaeology is Erich von Däniken, whose 1968 work *Chariots of the Gods?* promotes the theory of ancient human civilisations making contracts with more technologically advanced extra-terrestrial civilizations. Publications of this nature often reject well-established theories with limited evidence and are guilty of interpreting evidence with a preconceived theory in mind.

Such theories tend to compound the faulty assumption that prehistoric people were stupid or savages. A good archaeologist never refers to a society as *primitive* due to it being an *ethnocentric* term – judging a culture based on the values of your own. Just because past societies used simpler technology and social organisation, it does not mean they were stupid. For example, prior to the advent of writing people would have needed to remember all their accumulated knowledge in their heads in order to pass it on accurately to the next generation – and this might have made them *smarter*.

Looters

Yet another myth surrounding archaeology is that it is centred on artefacts. Artefacts are merely a means of finding out information about past people, and any object – no matter how glamorous – that lacks an archaeological context is scientifically useless.

People who dig purely to find artefacts rather than study them are called *looters* by archaeologists. It is unethical to buy and sell irreplaceable artefacts (they should be donated to museums to be conserved and studied for the benefit of the public), and looters are responsible for destroying the scientific value of archaeological sites (e.g. by failing to record the context of artefacts) in their quest for personal gain.

Measurements

Almost all archaeological work in the present day is carried out using the metric system because of its status as the world standard for scientific study.

There are, however, exceptions to this general rule. For example, when working on sites where objects or buildings were deliberately constructed in feet and inches, it makes more sense to measure them using these units.

Culture and Material Culture

The term *culture* refers to the ideas, customs and social behaviour of a particular people or society. Obviously this cannot be excavated, but we can use their *material culture* (the physical remains they left behind) to find clues about their beliefs and behaviour. These remains can be broadly classified as *artefacts*, *ecofacts* and *features*.

Artefacts and Ecofacts

Archaeological finds can be broadly divided into two categories: *artefacts* (man-made products) and *ecofacts* (natural objects that help the landscape and environment surrounding an archaeological site to be understood).

Any object shaped by human activity is an artefact, and can include things as large as a temple (which is composed of lots of individual artefacts), pottery, or even stones used to chip and shape arrowheads. In the majority of cases artefacts are portable objects that can be removed from the archaeological site and studied in a laboratory.

Ecofacts, on the other hand, are natural objects used by humans without modification. This could include pollen from gathered plants or discarded animal bones from dinner (which would be an artefact if sharpened to make a harpoon point).

What counts as a 'find' varies depending on the nature of the site and the excavation strategy. Some sites contain so many finds that they have to be taken away in a large vehicle – known as *common* or *bulk* finds. In such instances, a basic record is kept of the material (e.g. quantity and weight), but only *special* finds (e.g. because they are intact, or contain graffiti or a thumb print, etc.) are kept.

At the other end of the spectrum, there are some sites that contain so little archaeological material that archaeologists aim to salvage even the most insubstantial finds.

Features

Anything made by humans that is too large to bring to the laboratory intact is classified as a *feature*. This could include graves, roads, hearths, garbage pits and *postmold*s (where posts formerly stood in the ground).

In some cases it might be possible to cut out a block of soil around a feature and transport it to a laboratory, but more often than not features have to be excavated, studied and preserved where they are discovered.

Context

A *context* is the association of artefacts and features found within an area or layer, and the relative position and relationship of this area or layer to the ones above it and below it. This is used to interpret archaeological finds and understand their function and meaning.

Sites

An archaeological site is a place where human activity has taken place and artefacts, ecofacts or features can be found. They can come in many shapes and sizes, and – depending on what's preserved – can be small or large and shallow or deep. New *components* are added to a site when people of one time period use a place that has previously be used by people from an earlier time period. Some multicomponent sites can contain cultural deposits dating back thousands of years – with one component overlying the next. In the ideal site there is a culturally sterile layer between each component making it easy to distinguish one component from another. Unfortunately, this is rarely the case, with later occupants digging into the site and – in so doing – mixing their own material with the material of previous occupants.

Site formations

The development of an archaeological site can take place over very long or very brief periods of time and as a result of large or small human actions. Archaeologists refer to this process as *site formation*, and it is divided into two categories: *cultural* and *natural* processes.

Cultural processes that contribute to the formation of an archaeological site broadly include all human activity that creates material evidence. Here are some examples:

- **Finding raw materials and creating artefacts.** This can include making everything from simple stone tools to temples, as well as the waste that results from their production.
- **Leaving traces of activity.** Leaving any marks or debris where a particular activity was performed, such as repairing things, moving things, and using material items and physical spaces.
- **Discarding items.** This can happen deliberately or by accident and includes rubbish dumps, and storing items and forgetting about them.

- **Reusing things.** This could include taking apart old tombs to use the building blocks for new construction projects.
- **Disturbing ground containing archaeological material.** This could include ploughing or bulldozing sites to make way for new construction.

Natural processes also have a big role to play in the formation of archaeological sites, including:

- **Physical processes**, such as wind, rain, volcanoes, and other climatic conditions.
- **Biological processes**, such as bacteria (or other organisms that cause decay) and animals burrowing.
- **Chemical processes**, such as decomposing plants and animals in acidic soils, rusting iron, and weathering stone.

All these processes outlined above help to shape the way any given site appears or is composed of. They can be on a small scale (an iron artefact rusting beyond recognition) or on a large scale (volcanic ash covering the Roman city of Pompeii), and they can be destructive (causing organic materials to decay) or contribute to the site's preservation (as is the case with Pompeii).

Where do archaeologists dig?

It is easy to fall into the trap of thinking archaeological work is easy – just grab a shovel and a metal detector and start digging.

In reality, archaeology is a precise science that needs to be executed with rigorous accuracy to be successful in finding what you're looking for.

Assuming anyone who can wield a shovel can excavate is also false. Just like a surgeon with a scalpel, archaeological excavations require a great deal of patience and the use of expert techniques to prevent damaging the evidence. Unlike other sciences, archaeology – regretfully – destroys its subject matter in the process of investigating it, and therefore demands great skill and diligent record-keeping.

The History of Archaeology

According to historical records, the first person to dig up remains of their society's past and restore and display them was a Babylonian king in the 6th century BC called Nabonidus.

Dubbed the world's first archaeologist, Nabonidus led some of the earliest excavations in human history, culminating in the discovery of the foundation deposits of the temples of the sun god Šamaš, the warrior goddess Anunitu (both located in Sippar), and the sanctuary that Naram-Sin built to the moon god Sin (located in Harran). He also had them restored to their former glory, and is also credited as being the first person to attempt to date an archaeological artefact while searching for Naram-Sin's temple. And even though his estimate proved to be inaccurate by about 1,500 years, it was still a very good one considering the lack of accurate dating technology at the time.

Nevertheless, real archaeology can only be traced as far back as the Renaissance (14th to 17th centuries AD), when there was a revival in Classical learning and a multi-disciplinary study known as *antiquarianism* emerged.

In the 15th century the Italian humanist Flavio Biondo created a systematic guide to the ruins and topography of ancient Rome (earning him the status as an early founder of archaeology), and in the 16th century the English antiquarians John Leland and William Camden conducted surveys of the English countryside – drawing and interpreting any monuments they encountered.

During this period, wealthy aristocrats travelled to the ruins of ancient civilisations such as Mesopotamia, Egypt, Greece and Rome, and collected antiquities recovered from these ruins. By the

18th century antiquarian societies and collectors had amassed a large number of artefacts and began to display them in museums.

An *antiquarian*, therefore, is essentially someone who studies history through ancient artefacts and manuscripts. They relied on empirical evidence to understand the past, as emphasised by the 18th century antiquarian Sir Richard Colt Hoare when he wrote: 'We speak from facts not theory.'

Early excavations

Some notable early excavations include Stonehenge in the 1620s (prompted by a visit by King James I) and Pompeii and Herculaneum in the mid-18th century (when the Spanish military engineer Roque Joaquín de Alcubierre discovered architectural remains).

However, in an age before modern scientific techniques, excavations were typically poorly conducted and the vital importance of concepts such as stratification and context were overlooked.

19th century archaeology

By the early 1800s, a sufficient quantity of artefacts had been recovered to interpret the human past in an orderly manner; using historical models to track the progress of human society over time.

Early classification efforts were guided by two prominent Danes.

The antiquarian Christian Thomsen (1788-1865) organised finds at Denmark's national museum, and divided them into three 'ages' of human development: the Stone Age, the Bronze Age, and the Iron Age.

Meanwhile, the archaeologist Jens Worsaae (1821-85) discovered that stone tools were the deepest (and therefore the oldest), followed by bronze and iron tools respectively while conducting excavations – proving Thomsen's three-age system.[6]

The Stone Age would later be sub-divided into the Old (Palaeolithic) and New (Neolithic) Stone Age, and these classifications continue to be used today with some notable changes:

- Each age occurred at different times in different parts of the world.
- It is wrong to refer to human 'progress' or 'stages of development' seeing as there is no such thing as a single path of human development. Different cultures change and become more or less complex over time in different ways.
- Such cultural classifications are centred on technology and fail to acknowledge other important elements of human development (e.g. in art, literature, architecture and religion).

Many early archaeologists sought excitement and adventure by seeking out ancient remains and artefacts. And although they did not *discover* sites (because local people were almost always aware of their existence), good archaeologists published their findings and brought the antiquities home for public display. For example, the Rosetta Stone was unearthed by Napoleon's men during their 1798 invasion of Egypt. Containing the same inscription written in Ancient Greek and two Ancient Egyptian scripts, Demotic and hieroglyphs, the French scholar Jean-François Champollion was eventually able to decode the writing systems of Ancient Egypt.[7]

Unfortunately many of Champollion's contemporaries did not follow his example and used antiquities for the selfish purposes of financial gain or to display as a status symbol on their own private estates. By the end of the 19th century, however, archaeological work had become increasingly scientific thanks to an increased awareness of the need for systematic study to make sense of the wealth of finds being unearthed.

One of the first scientific-minded archaeologists was Augustus Pitt Rivers (1827-1900), whose work was highly methodical by the standards of the time. He insisted that *all* artefacts, not just those that were aesthetically pleasing, should be collected and catalogued. This recognition of the importance of everyday objects to understanding the past helped to undermine previous archaeological practices which had bordered on treasure hunting.

Similarly, the Egyptologist Flinders Petrie (1853-1942) wrote 'I believe the true line of research lies in the noting and comparison of the smallest details.' He revolutionised the chronological basis of Egyptology by developing a system of dating layers based on pottery and ceramic findings, and trained and mentored an entire generation of Egyptologists – including the most famous of all, Howard Carter.

Early 20th century archaeology

While jaw-dropping discoveries continued to be made in the 20th century, more orderly forms of excavation became increasingly common. Archaeology was primarily a hobby for the wealthy, who had the free time and financial means to travel to exotic locales, but it also became a professional activity that could be studied at universities and even schools.

One of the most famous discoveries made during this period was the discovery of the tomb of Tutankhamun by the English archaeologist Howard Carter (1874-1939), who had been sponsored by George Herbert, Earl of Carnarvon (1866-1923) to explore the Valley of the Kings. Although a relatively unimportant New Kingdom pharaoh, Tutankhamun's tomb became famous for being left untouched by looters.

Other famous excavations included the work of Sir Leonard Woolley (1880-1960) in the Mesopotamian city-state of Ur, who is recognised as one of the first 'modern' archaeologists: excavating in a methodical manner, keeping careful records, and using them to reconstruct the human past.

Meanwhile, the Australian archaeologist Vere Gordon Childe (1892-1957) began to organise the vast amounts of information digs were yielding by producing the first major synthesis of prehistory. Known as the 'great synthesiser' for his work integrating regional research with a broader picture of Near Eastern and European prehistory, he emphasised the role of revolutionary technological and economic developments in human society. This includes the Neolithic Revolution (the widespread transition of numerous human cultures during the Neolithic period from a hunter-gatherer lifestyle to one centred on agriculture and settlement, making population growth possible) and the Urban Revolution (the process by which small, kin-based, non-literate agricultural villages were transformed into large, socially complex, urban societies).

'New Archaeology' and the mid-20th century

In the aftermath of World War Two a mini-revolution occurred in the archaeological field, facilitated by wartime technological advances and a general desire to be more scientific.

Many archaeologists became dissatisfied with merely describing and cataloguing what they found and where (known as *culture history*), and sought to gain a better understanding of how past human cultures functioned.

This movement was branded *new archaeology* at the time (but is now known as *processual archaeology*). It had a number of influences, including:

- New technology (e.g. computers and aerial photography).
- Scientific advances (e.g. radiocarbon dating).
- A growing awareness of the importance of preserving historic sites and safeguarding them against development and industrial farming.

One of the first works of new archaeology was the 1958 book *Method and Theory in American Archaeology* by the American archaeologists Gordon Willey (1913-2002) and Philip Phillips (1900-94). In this work, Willey and Phillips argued that the goals of archaeology are the same as those of anthropology – to answer questions about humans and human society. In so doing they criticised the former period of culture-historical archaeology, which merely described and classified artefacts rather than using them to find out information about past people and ways of life.

Late 20th century archaeology

A couple of decades after the founding of new archaeology, it was rebranded *processual archaeology* – after the method exploring cultural processes.

To this day, the majority of archaeological work falls under processual archaeology, although post-processual archaeology (which also contributes a great deal to present-day archaeology) was established in the United Kingdom in the late 1970s and early 1980s – criticising scientific archaeology for being too ethnocentric and biased in favour of the dominant culture.[8] Within the post-processualist movement, a wide variety of theoretical viewpoints have been embraced, including structuralism[9] and Neo-Marxism[10], as have a variety of different archaeological techniques, such as phenomenology.[11]

21st century archaeology

Today, many laws protect archaeological remains and ensure greater archaeological investigation takes place prior to development.

Archaeologists are expected to combine the descriptive nature of culture history with scientific approaches and an awareness of any biases that might appear in their research. They also need to be aware of issues relating to heritage (e.g. whose ancestors are you digging up?), the political side to archaeology (e.g. promoting someone's land claims) and conservation (preventing the destruction of archaeological sites).

One of the greatest shifts of all moving into the 21st century, however, is the growing acknowledgement that all archaeology is public archaeology. In the space of a century, the discipline has gone from being an aristocratic hobby to an academic field that seeks to understand changes in human nature over time – with such work often being funded by the public and being regarded as part of a collective human heritage.

Types of Archaeology

Like almost all academic disciplines, there are many different types of archaeology you can specialise in. These sub-disciplines can be defined by a range of things, including a specific method or type of material (e.g. lithic analysis and archaeobotany), a geographical or chronological focus (e.g. Near Eastern and Medieval), other thematic concerns (e.g. maritime archaeology and landscape archaeology), or a specific culture or civilization (e.g. Egyptology, Indology and Sinology).

Scientific and humanistic elements in archaeology

Archaeology is both a social science and part of the humanities.

Archaeologists normally use the scientific method of devising hypotheses based on what they find and then testing them on subsequent digs using *empirical* (observable) evidence.

Humanistic study, meanwhile, also comes to the fore when determining what artefacts meant to past peoples and what they valued, felt and thought. For example, one humanistic question might be – 'What did a cultural group believe that compelled them to construct such lavish tombs and perform sacrificial rituals?' From this, more questions will emerge, such as 'What did sacrificial victims think about their fate – honoured or reluctant?'

Humanistic models of the human past cannot normally be tested scientifically, but involve imagination and have the potential to broaden your ways of viewing the past. They work best when conducting historic archaeology, seeing as written records give some idea of what the past people being studied thought.

In most cases archaeologists combine scientific and humanistic approaches, although this can vary depending on the individual's theoretical and philosophical views, as well as on the sizes of their budgets and who is funding their work.

Regional specialisation

Some archaeologists become so enamoured by working in a particular area of the world (for example, Mesoamerica) that they choose to specialise in archaeological work there. Some regional archaeology, such as Egyptian archaeology, has become so popular that it even has its own name – Egyptology.

Period specialisation

Some archaeologists fall in love with a specific time period in human history, and become experts at identifying its typical artefacts and establishing how people lived. An example of this kind of specialisation is Palaeolithic archaeologists, who know all about stone tools (which was the main material people had to work with at the time), including how the stone was obtained and shaped.

Artefact or site specialisation

Some archaeologists are particularly interested in specific types of artefacts, including:

- *Lithic* (the Greek word for 'stone') experts closely study the development of stone tools throughout history, and even learn how to make them.
- *Cordage* (string or yarn) experts specialise in studying preserved fibre fragments and the imprints of cords and fabrics on clay.
- *Pottery* experts study the designs, dimensions and composition of different forms of ceramics – establishing which types were characteristics of certain regions and time periods.

Other archaeologists are more interested in working on specific sites, including:

- Sites where stone has been quarried are particularly popular with lithic experts, as they can be gold mines for chipped pieces of stone and discarded tools.
- Sites containing rock art require an expertise in things such as pigments and rock types.
- Stunning architecture such as pyramids, mounds, monuments and temples have long been go-to sites for archaeologists. In order to study them properly, the archaeologist needs an understanding of a whole host of things including engineering, architecture and perhaps even astronomy.

Many of these varieties of archaeology can overlap each other, and vary depending on what you're looking for and why, as well as on what you find.

Anthropology

In North America, archaeology is part of anthropology, which studies humans from biological and cultural perspectives. It is broadly divided into four fields:

Cultural and Social Anthropology: studies living cultures.

Biological (or Physical) Anthropology: studies the evolution of human beings over millions of years, and the genetic and physical variations amongst humans in the present day.

Linguistic Anthropology: studies how languages evolve and their relationship with culture.

Archaeology: is the only branch of anthropology that does not require people. Instead of using living people's actions to find out about past behaviour, archaeologists use the remains they left behind.

Applied anthropology: is sometimes added as a fifth sub-discipline. It refers to applying the methods and findings of anthropology for use in the modern world.

Sub-disciplines

Some sub-disciplines of archaeology include…

Prehistoric Archaeology: includes everything that happened in the human past before writing was invented, and therefore encompasses almost everything people have ever done – inventing artefacts, organising societies, developing culture and belief systems, etc. Prehistorians reconstruct the deep human past based on what they find. They need to have an understanding of historic cultures that descend from the prehistoric people being studied, although only loose comparisons should be made to known cultures.

Historical Archaeology: deals with past cultures where some form of writing can inform and contextualise cultural material. Such studies, therefore, focus on literate, historic societies as opposed to non-literate, prehistoric societies, and can both complement and conflict with the archaeological evidence found at a particular site.

Unlike prehistoric archaeology, then (which ventures back millions of years), historic archaeology can only be used to study societies up to around 3,000-5,000 years old when the first writing was developed.

Despite written records giving archaeologists a better idea of what they're digging up, they can have their problems. Some include:

- History is normally written by the victors, resulting in either bias reports or little attention being paid to conquered peoples.

- In many past societies only a select few people from a certain social class could write, resulting in it reflecting their biases and leaving many groups in society unrepresented.
- Writing was used for different purposes in different cultures.
- Written records began at different times in different places. For example, North America lacks written records prior to its 'discovery' by European explorers and colonists in the late 15th century.

Underwater Archaeology: is far more expensive and time consuming than archaeology on land. In addition, you have to tackle the obstacles of water pressure, tides, currents, poor visibility and even sharks.

Though often mistaken as such, underwater archaeology is not restricted to the study of shipwrecks. Changes in sea level because of local seismic events (such as the earthquakes that devastated Port Royal and Alexandria) or more widespread climatic changes on a continental scale mean that some sites of human occupation that were once on dry land are now submerged.

Some examples of underwater sites and sub-disciplines include:

- *Marine* (or *maritime*) *archaeology* involves the study of sites related to seafaring cultures and human interaction with the sea, lakes and rivers. This can include the study of a range of physical remains, such as shipwrecks, ports, shore-side facilities, cargo, human remains and submerged landscapes.
- *Nautical archaeology* particularly focuses on ship-building and watercraft.
- *Prehistoric* or *historic underwater archaeology* investigates sites now submerged due to rising sea

levels since the end of the Pleistocene (Ice Age).

Underwater archaeology is a relatively recent phenomena due to the countless difficulties of accessing and working on underwater sites.

Classical Archaeology: deals with the Mediterranean civilizations of Ancient Greece and Ancient Rome. Essentially a sub-discipline of historical archaeology, it can involve studying the art, architecture or writings of these societies.

Forensic Archaeology: is the specialist application of archaeological techniques to the search and recovery of evidence from crime scenes, often (but not always) related to buried human remains. This can be used to provide accurate and clear evidence in legal and law enforcement cases, as well as to assist in international investigations of genocide and mass murder. Working for the United Nations or other humanitarian organisations, archaeologists excavate graves of missing people (who could be the victims of state crimes, warfare, plane crashes or natural disasters) and locate and identify remains for relatives of victims.

Ethnoarchaeology: is where archaeologists study the material and non-material traditions of living human societies to help them interpret the archaeological record and in turn reconstruct ancient lifeways. Ethnographic studies are a good way of understanding how objects were made and what they were used for, and work particularly well with hunter-gatherer societies, because you can follow them as they use tools, catch animals and perform other activities.

The approach emerged in the 1960s along with the processual movement, and continues to be a prominent component of many present-day archaeological approaches. For it to be of any use, however, there needs to be some sort of continuity between the past culture you're trying to interpret and the present-day culture you're observing.

Experimental Archaeology: attempts to test archaeological hypotheses, typically by replicating or gauging the feasibility of past cultures performing various tasks or feats. One of the most common forms of this type of archaeology is constructing replicas of historical structures using only historically accurate technologies (sometimes called *reconstruction archaeology*, although calling it a 'working construction of the past' would be more accurate seeing as the latter term implies one person's idea of the past rather than an exact replica).

*

Some sub-disciplines of archaeology require professional training in a second subject area…

Zooarchaeology: involves studying and identifying animal remains at archaeological sites, and essentially combines the studies of archaeology and zoology (the study of animals).

The most common faunal remains (items left behind when an animal dies) found at archaeological sites include bones and shells, although in the majority of cases these faunal remains do not survive – causing difficulties in identifying the remains and interpreting their significance.

Some things zooarchaeology can reveal about remains include:

- What species of animal are present at a site.
- What animals people were eating.
- Whether animals were being domesticated or hunted and captured wild.
- What the environment was like (e.g. based on what insects are found).
- What part of the animal's body a bone is from. From this you can obtain the *minimum number of individuals* (MNI) for each species at your site. For instance, if you

uncover two goat legs but both come from the front left leg, you know there were at least two goats at the site.

- Calculate how much meat you can get from each type of animal using experimental archaeology. By de-fleshing the bones of roadkill and weighing the amount of meat each animal yields you can estimate how much each type of animal contributed to a past person's hypothetical diet. Be careful though. Animal bone remains do not always reveal everything the past people at a site might have been eating. For instance, they might have thrown fish bones straight back into the river rather than into their waste piles due to the smell.

Paleoethnobotany: is the study of plant remains at archaeological sites. Through this paleoethnobotanists can find out a wealth of information about things such as past diets, domestication and environments, as well as determine what resources were used for what purpose (e.g. medical plants for drugs or plants used in industry like cotton). These are similar things you can tell from animal bones and shells, but plants are far more delicate and are only normally preserved if they are waterlogged, charred or dried.

Macrobotanical remains are larger plant remains such as nuts, seeds, corn cobs, charcoal from fires and fragments of wood. These finds can then be compared with what types of plants are found in the region surrounding the site to work out what plants were naturally occurring at the site, what plants people grew there, and what plants were imported from further afield.

Microbotanical remains, on the other hand, are much smaller plant remains that require a microscope to see. This could include pollen grains, which have a unique shape for each plant species. By using this to work out the plant's characteristics you can also work out what the past environment looked like. But be careful to make sure you know how much pollen each plant produces. Different plants release different amounts of pollen, so just because there is more pollen from one species than another it doesn't mean that it was predominant in the area. In addition to this, on-site pollen should be compared with off-site pollen to determine what was natural to the area and what people were bringing in.[12]

Microscopic mineral deposits that form within plant cells called *phytoliths* are also incredibly useful to archaeologists. Like pollen, they have distinct shapes based on what species of plant they formed within and often survive long after the plant itself has decayed. By separating them from the soil using complicated methods, archaeologists have been able to use phytoliths to see how early plants (such as corn) were domesticated by past people.

Archaeometry: or *archaeological science* involves the application of scientific techniques to analyse and date archaeological materials. It often focuses on the chemical composition of archaeological remains and investigates spatial characteristics of features (using methods such as space syntax techniques and geodesy, as well as computerised tools such as geographic information systems). Its uses include dating materials, working out what artefacts are composed of, and tracing their origins.

Bioarchaeology: involves studying human bones and can be used to estimate the age and gender of a person using skeletal markers (especially the pelvis). In addition to this, marks left on the bones can reveal stress from hard labour and the presence of certain injuries or diseases, and the length of a person's arm or leg can be used to estimate the person's height. Dental cavities offer an insight into the diet and hygiene of the deceased and signs of cultural practices such as foot-binding or head-flattening can also be seen.

Even more information can be found from conducting studies into the chemical makeup of bones. While a person's teeth might contain minerals from the water they drank as a child, bones that formed later on in life contain minerals from where they were living closer to their time of death. By investigating the minerals in the water and soil of different regions, then, you can work out where a person was born and raised in comparison to where they lived when they died. Alternatively, by subjecting bone collagen to *stable carbon isotope analysis* traces of different types of plants can sometimes be found which reveal what plants they were eating and whether they were domesticated or gathered in the wild.

A more ethical option, however, would be to use ancient dried faeces known as *coprolites* (if it can be identified as human) to search for information about past peoples' diets, health, environments (from accidentally ingested insects) and the extent of domestication.

In some cases (such as in mummified remains) there is enough soft tissue preserved to use CAT scans and X-rays to find out about the diseases and traumas the person suffered from in life, and perhaps even their cause of death.

*

In addition to archaeological fields, the nature of your projects and how you interpret your finds are influenced by a multitude of philosophical frameworks. In present-day archaeology a combination of these frameworks are used, with *culture history* being used to establish what happened before using scientific methods (*processual archaeology*) to answer questions about these cultural processes and *postprocessual* methods to reveal the biases and weaknesses of science.

Culture History: is purely descriptive – saying what, when and where something happened. This involves describing archaeological remains and what they reveal about past human activity. You then produce succeeding cultures through time, with their characteristic artefacts and ways of life. This approach to archaeology dominated the field until the second half of the 20th century, when the importance of scientific methods began to be highlighted.

Processual Archaeology: emerged in the 1960s and 1970s and claims the rigorous use of scientific methods can help overcome the limits of the archaeological record and to learn something about how the people who used the artefacts lived. Particular perspectives within processual archaeology include *middle-range theory* (where you seek to find casual links between the archaeological evidence and past human activity responsible for its creation) and *cultural materialism* (where you regard past human cultures as being predominantly shaped by the limits of the material world, such as the environment, the economy and technology. In the case of archaeology, explaining culture in terms of material conditions is ideal because material remains are what archaeologists have to work with).

Processual archaeology came into being after archaeologists became increasingly dissatisfied with merely describing archaeological finds and past cultures, rather than asking important questions about how past cultures operated, why they changed or stayed the same, etc.

Postprocessual Archaeology: was a response to the limitations of processual archaeology, and emerged in the 1980s and 1990s. It emphasises the subjectivity of archaeological interpretations, studying past cultures using humanistic (philosophy and speculation) rather than empirical (scientific) means. Cultures and individuals are regarded as acting in different ways, and therefore any attempt at establishing universal laws about human cultural systems and behaviour is futile. Interpreting the past using speculative non-scientifically testable means is acceptable, while the claim of scientists that everything is knowable is dismissed.

Processual archaeology has many variations, including:

- *Agency theory*: Where powerful individuals are regarded as being the primary drivers of cultural change, rather than people being at the mercy of environmental or economic factors. The decisions of past leaders are easier to study in historic archaeology, because written records give you a much better idea of who has a hold on power and how they acquired/maintained it.

- *Cognitive archaeology*: Where you seek to determine the ideologies of past people. This is easier when conducting historic archaeology, because written sources provide you with a good starting point for interpreting what people thought and believed.

- *Critical theory*: Where you acknowledge both open and hidden biases in scientific interpretations of the past (including racism, sexism and ethnocentrism).
- *Feminist archaeology*: Where you focus on gender roles in past societies as well as amending bias male interpretations.
- *Marxist archaeology*: Where you interpret past human behaviour in terms of Marxist theory – centred on control over resources and the means of production.
- *Reflexive archaeology*: Where you acknowledge your interpretation of the past – far from being the gospel truth – is merely one of many possible explanations. This allows you to keep an open mind and to view your data in different ways.
- *Symbolic and structural archaeology*: Where you interpret how people thought in the past by studying how symbols are organised. This is based on the assumption that all humans have similar thought processes and that their structure is reflected in symbols. This method is only normally effective with historic archaeology.

Historic Preservation and Public Archaeology

All countries have laws in some shape or form aimed at protecting historic and archaeological sites – on public land at the very least. Historic preservation specialists might work for government agencies, private companies or even as lobbyists to improve legislation or raise money to protect sites.

Cultural Resources Management (CRM)

A large amount of archaeological work in the present day is dedicated to locating and saving remains of the human past so they can be investigated.

In archaeological jargon, significant historic artefacts, buildings and sites are *cultural resources. Managing* them, meanwhile, entails deciding how to protect and study them.

The first stage of cultural resources management (CRM), then, is to find the sites as well as to be aware of any relevant laws. After this, you can decide how to interpret the sites to the public and whether they are important enough to be preserved or expendable to development.

Some archaeologists responsible for managing cultural resources work for the government, but they are more frequently hired as *contract archaeologists* – surveying and locating sites before assessing their importance.

Contract Archaeology

The majority of archaeological work today is carried out in the form of *contract archaeology*, funded by university departments, private companies and non-profit organisations.

Contract archaeology is usually motivated by profit, and should technically be carried out with the same high research standards used in other forms of archaeology. However, that is easier said than done seeing as many clients want the work doing fast and on tight budgets – giving rise to even more ethical concerns than other archaeologists face.

Typically, contract archaeology is composed of three stages:

- **Survey:** Use the records of a planned construction project to see if any known sites fall inside the development area, before conducting fieldwork to locate any unrecorded sites. In some cases a *reconnaissance survey* is used (which isn't as in-depth as a full survey). This could mean having a brief walk over the project area or only checking existing records, rather than conducting a detailed field inspection or shovel tests (mini excavations) to find out what is buried. If nothing important is found, archaeological work could cease at this stage. However, the discovery of significant archaeological remains could result in the planned development being altered to avoid them.
- **Test excavation:** Sometimes a limited excavation is required to evaluate the importance of a site. For example, if artefacts are found on the surface of the site, test excavations may be dug (perhaps a metre square) to see if any intact *cultural deposits* (undisturbed layers containing signs of past human activity, such as artefacts) are there.
- **Excavations:** Sites of high importance might still have to be destroyed in the name of development. In this instance, *rescue archaeology* (also known as *salvage archaeology* or *data recovery*) will be carried out, where much bigger areas are excavated so it can be studied as comprehensively as possible before it is destroyed.

Curation and Museums

There are many elements to museum work, and it can range from raising funds to giving tours to producing exhibitions.

When doing any of these things, it is essential to have a sound knowledge of archaeological theory to prevent the reconstruction of past people's lives being distorted by modern values and biases, as well as an understanding of ethics and antiquities laws (e.g. to avoid acquiring looted artefacts and becoming part of the problem).

A large part of museum work involves curation and collections management.

Curation means taking care of things. In the case of museums, the first phase of curation involves cleaning, numbering and analysing archaeological finds following an excavation. But that's only the beginning of the hard work, because after this artefacts and their data must be stored to ensure:

- They do not decay.
- They are clearly listed in an easy-to-understand catalogue.
- You never lose information concerning their provenience (the location where they were originally found).
- They are stored in suitable conditions – e.g. away from humid air, termites, rats and burglars; and kept in sturdy, non-degradable containers.
- They can be easily located for research purposes.
- They can be accessed for display in public exhibitions.

Public archaeology

Also known as *community archaeology*, public archaeology is archaeology by the people for the people and can include any of the following:

- Archaeological investigations conducted with public funding or support.
- Archaeological investigations conducted in a public setting.
- Archaeological investigations involving members of the public, including *amateur* or *avocational archaeology* (where people do it as a hobby, under the supervision of professionals).
- Archaeological investigations involving communities or individuals who descend from the past people being studied.
- Community heritage archaeology (where past people are linked to the current inhabitants of the area, regardless of relation).
- Cultural resources management (CRM)
- Your investigation's findings are available in popular formats (such as in newspapers or online).
- Educational archaeology
- Museum exhibitions
- Archaeotourism (where you promote public interest in archaeology by making archaeological sites, museums and re-enactments open to tourists. In theory this will generate revenue and help to fund conservation efforts).
- Applied anthropology (using archaeological knowledge to help solve problems in the present-day).

In addition to this, potential *stakeholders* (individuals or groups interested in your archaeological investigation) might include:

- The general public

- Fellow archaeologists
- The landowner(s)
- Local residents

- Individuals or groups who descend from (or claim to descend from) the past people being studied.
- People interested in your investigation for ulterior motives, such as to promote tourism or block a planned development.
- Looters

In almost all archaeological investigations you should try to find a way of involving the public. Local residents and knowledgeable volunteers can be of great use in a range of settings – digging on site, processing finds back at the lab or publicising the investigation – and it is only fair that you keep them up to date on what your project has achieved.

Here are some ways you could present your findings to the public:

- Give talks about the investigation in the local community – at schools, universities, libraries, etc.

- Write a press release for the media to ensure all news reports on the project are accurate.
- Write an investigation report aimed at the general public, in addition to the professional one you submit to the organisation who funded your research. You might even want to create a website, giving regular updates on the progress of the project.

Archaeology and Politics

Arguments over what happened in the past and who controls archaeological finds are never-ending, such as the ongoing dispute between Greece and the British Museum over who should possess the Elgin Marbles. Archaeology is constantly being revised with new and often contradictory interpretations of the past – and in many cases it is exploited by individuals or groups to invent claims to power by associating themselves with significant archaeological sites or artefacts. Therefore, you should always anticipate disagreement when conducting archaeological work and make an effort to locate and contact any interested parties to try to settle any potential arguments that your project might spark.

Collectors and Looters

Some stakeholders in archaeological work are interested in collecting artefacts, and fall into two broad categories: *ethical collectors* and *looters*.

Ethical collectors (also known as avocational or amateur archaeologists) collect artefacts as a hobby while ensuring they keep a record of the provenience of their finds and are happy to share their information and artefacts with professional archaeologists. In other words, the work of ethical collectors helps to advance collective archaeological knowledge.

Looters (or pothunters), on the other hand, collect artefacts for personal gain (either to display or sell on the black market). They do not care what information they can provide about past human societies and therefore do not bother recording the provenience of their finds or allow professionals to study them. Archaeological resources belong to everyone, and therefore the buying and selling of artefacts is regarded as highly unethical by professional archaeologists. In addition to this, many laws have been enacted by governments around the world to prevent the illegal trafficking of antiquities. The most significant international agreement concerning looting is the 'UNESCO Convention on the Means of Prohibiting and Preventing the Illicit Import, Export and Transfer of Ownership of Cultural Property'. Currently ratified by 140 countries, it allows member nations to recover illegally exported antiquities from other member nations.

Practical application

One of archaeology's biggest contributions to the present-day is showing how people shaped and were affected by their environment in the long-term. This can include shedding light on how people adapted to environmental change, how they exploited resources, and how they learned to live in a variety of regions – from deserts to wetlands to mountains to rainforests. Or it might reveal how human actions have contributed to the destruction of ecosystems or, by stark contrast, succeeded in managing their natural resources sustainably (and thus secured the longevity of their society).

You might even be able to rediscover past human technology that has uses in the present-day, such as ways of harnessing wind and water power to produce renewable energy, and determining how different waste disposal techniques used by different societies have impacted the environment and landscape in the long-term.

Archaeological Research

All archaeological investigations begin with the researcher determining what they're looking for and why, as well as how they intend to go about finding it.

Once this has been established they can begin to make other key decisions, including how many workers and what equipment will be needed, how much it will cost, how long it will take, and what techniques and specialist studies will be used.

Archaeology stresses *conservation* over *digging* (which destroys the archaeological record), and so a strong justification (such as finding answers to well-thought-out questions that cannot be obtained by any other means) is needed to disturb sites.

Some reasons for conducting archaeological investigations include:

- Finding out something specific about the past (e.g. how old a stone circle is or why it was erected).
- Uncovering archaeological evidence to help reconstruct the story of an area where little is known about its past.
- Establishing the past functions of a site.
- Determining if a site is worth saving when threatened by development.
- Recovering specific types of remains.

Even though you should know in advance of an excavation what you're looking for, they are hard to plan because unexpected finds are often made. This could result in the project's aims being adjusted mid-excavation.

Research Design

All archaeological projects – regardless of whether they are a *survey* (searching for sites) or an *excavation* (digging sites) – need a *research design.*

These are documents used in scientific studies to detail what you're looking for, what your plan is to find it, as well as guiding your work and justifying why you're doing it in the first place.

Some things you should include in a research design are:

- The aim of the research (normally stated in terms of scientific hypotheses you want to test).
- The *methodology* (what methods are needed to achieve the research aims).
- Logistical details (e.g. how many people are participating and how long the project will last).
- Verification that required permits have been obtained from the government and/or landowners to allow the dig to proceed.
- What results you anticipate and how you plan to respond to unexpected finds.
- What will happen to the site once the excavation has been completed.
- How information and finds recovered from the site will be analysed.
- Where and how the finds, notes and records produced by the dig will be stored for future researchers.

Be prepared for the high likelihood of the ideal project being undermined – by budget cuts, volunteers failing to turn up, equipment breakdowns, poor weather conditions, etc.

And on top of this there is the potential for your research questions to change as the project progresses – for example, as a result of uncovering different finds from what you were expecting.

Scientific method

In archaeology scientific methods do not *prove* things like you might imagine – they are merely used to support or reject hypotheses.

Broadly speaking, the scientific method is composed of the following steps:

- Ask a question about something that can be observed.
- Gather background information (what's already known about it).
- Devise potential explanations (or *hypotheses*) that can be tested.
- Test the hypotheses by collecting data. If the evidence refutes a hypothesis, start looking for a new explanation; if the evidence supports a hypothesis, it is good practice to test it again using different methods and a greater amount of data to refine the explanation.
- If the hypotheses are still supported, they can be used to create a whole model about how something works.

Key stages of archaeological investigations

Archaeological investigations are normally composed of several distinct stages, the most prominent being:

- A clear objective for what the project seeks to achieve must be established.
- A site survey is completed to find out as much as possible about the site and its surrounding area.
- If necessary, an excavation might take place to uncover buried archaeological material.
- The information gathered during the excavation is analysed in an attempt to achieve the research goals.
- Lastly, it is good practice to publish the findings so the information is available to help future researchers.

Remote sensing: refers to the acquisition of information about an object or phenomenon without making physical contact, and can be used prior to digging to see where sites are situated within a large area. This can include searching aerial photographs and satellite images for patterns on the ground.

There are two types of remote sensing instruments, *passive* and *active*; with the former detecting natural energy that is omitted or reflected from the scene being observed, and the latter emitting energy and recording what is reflected.

One example of passive remote sensing is satellite imagery, and two popular tools for active remote sensing are:

- *Lidar:* are mounted on aircraft and detect features on the ground by bouncing laser pulses off the earth.

In more technical language, they use a laser to transmit a light pulse and a receiver with sensitive detectors to measure backscattered (or reflected) light. By recording the time between the transmitted and backscattered pulses and calculating the distance travelled using the speed of light, the distance to the object can be measured.
It has many uses, including mapping features concealed by forest canopies or thick vegetation, and can produce high-resolution datasets quickly and cheaply. However, its effectiveness is severely limited in areas that do not reflect light pulses well – such as gravelly and peaty soils.[13]

- *Laser altimeters:* use a lidar to measure the height of the instrument platform above the surface. The topography beneath the surface can then be determined by knowing the height of the platform in relation to the Earth's mean surface.

In addition to this, there are a range of on-site remote sensing techniques. This is part of *geophysical prospecting* and involves moving various pieces of equipment across the site to get a better idea of what's buried in the soil before you proceed with the excavation. Some of these techniques involve using the following pieces of equipment:

- **Ground-penetrating radar (GPR)**
- **Magnetometers**
- **Electrical resistance meters**
- **Metal detectors**[14]

Even though remote sensing is a great way of finding out more about your site, in many instances the results are too ambiguous to identify what material is present without digging down to it.

Field survey: either serves as the beginning of an archaeological project or follows remote sensing (if it is used).

While *regional surveys* attempt to systematically locate previously unknown sites in a given region, *site surveys* attempt to systematically locate interesting features within a particular site.

Before the rise of processual archaeology in the late 20th century, surveys were not commonly used. Since then, however, it has proven its importance as a preliminary exercise to (or even a replacement for) excavation. Because large volumes of earth do not have to be processed to seek out artefacts, it is relatively cheap in terms of time and money, and because it does not damage the site it avoids ethical issues. It is also the only way of finding out some information, such as settlement patterns and structure, and survey data can be used to create maps – perhaps revealing the distribution of artefacts and surface features.

The most straightforward form of survey is known as a *surface survey*. This entails searching an area (on foot or by vehicle) for artefacts or features visible on the surface, although mini-excavation techniques such as augers, corers and shovel test pits might also be used. The main drawback of this technique is that it is unable to detect features that are buried or covered with vegetation.

Another way of carrying out a survey is an *aerial survey*, which uses cameras attached to aircraft, drones, balloons and kites. This bird's-eye view allows large or complex sites to be mapped quickly, and can also detect many things not visible from ground-level. As well as using ultraviolet, infrared, ground-penetrating radar wavelengths, Lidar and thermography, aerial photographs (when taken at different times of day) can detect the outlines of structures by changes in shadows as well as using changes in the colour of crops to reveal buried features. For example, while buried man-made structures will make plants above them grow at a slower rate, other features such as middens will make them develop faster.

Finally, *geophysical survey* is an effective way of seeing underground. The presence of features such as kilns, iron artefacts and ditches can be revealed by magnetometers, which detect minor deviations in the Earth's magnetic field. Any archaeological features that have a different electrical resistivity to the surrounding soil can be detected and mapped – with some features (including those composed of stone) having a higher resistivity than average soils and other features (including organic remains) typically having a lower resistivity.

Even metal detectors have a place. Although some archaeologists criticise their use as tantamount to treasure hunting, they can be put to good use in archaeological surveys. So long as metal detectorists keep detailed records of their results and avoid removing artefacts from their archaeological context, they have the potential to make important discoveries – such as their use in analysing musket ball distribution on American Civil War battlefields.

Excavation: is the most well-known aspect of archaeological work and the source of the majority of data recovered in field projects. It can reveal a wealth of information that cannot be acquired through survey, such as stratigraphy.

In present-day excavations it is essential to record the provenience (or precise location) of artefacts and features that are unearthed. To do this their horizontal position (and sometimes their vertical one) needs to be determined, as well as their relationship with nearby artefacts and features. This enables archaeologists to work out which artefacts and features were used together, and which ones are from different periods in the site's history.

Sampling is an important early step in the excavation process and sometimes requires large equipment (e.g. backhoes) to clear away the topsoil, before the exposed area is cleaned with hand-held tools (e.g. trowels) to see what features have been revealed.

After this a *site plan* needs to be devised to decide the excavation method.

Stakes and string are used to set out excavation units, and trowels continue to be the principal digging tool (as they have been for centuries).

Features dug into the natural subsoil (e.g. a ditch or pit) are typically excavated in sections to create a visible archaeological section that can be recorded. There are two parts to all features – the *cut* and the *fill* – and both are recorded by being assigned consecutive numbers. The *cut* refers to the edge of the feature (its boundary with the natural soil surrounding it), while the *fill* refers to what the feature is filled with (normally having a distinct appearance from the surrounding soil). As well as being photographed (in black and white), plans and sections of features are drawn to scale, and recording sheets are used to describe each individual feature's context. This serves as a permanent record of the archaeological material destroyed by the excavation, as well as being used to study and interpret the site.

Most fieldworkers carry a notebook to write down information such as how much they dig and what they find. A form is also filled in for each *level* (the arbitrary vertical amount you dig) or *stratum* (the visible natural or cultural soil layer you dig), and you may also be required to fill in forms describing the soil layering (*stratigraphy*), for certain features, and for photos taken during the excavation. Finds are listed in a daily field log, with the *provenience* recorded in the log and on the bag they are put inside.

Archaeologists usually leave areas unexcavated so that future researchers can examine the site again when new and improved methods are developed.

Some obvious issues concerning excavations are them being (relatively speaking) the most expensive part of an archaeological investigation, and ethical concerns such as its destructive impact on the site.

Analysis: is the most time-consuming part of an archaeological investigation. It involves studying artefacts and other material that has been recovered by surface surveys and excavations, and can take many years.

When subjected to a basic analysis, artefacts are cleaned, catalogued and compared to published collections (including classifying them typologically and identifying other sites with similar finds).

More complex analytical techniques can also be used, which allow the age and composition of finds to be examined.

Restoration and Reconstruction

Some archaeological investigations go a step further than seeking to investigate their past, and actually attempt to duplicate them through *restoration* or *reconstruction*.

While restoring a site might involve reassembling bricks and other remains to form their original structure, reconstruction involves building a new structure over the original's outline (often using the materials and methods that would have been used at the time).

Many museum and government funded excavations favour reconstruction so people can experience their local area's historical heritage first-hand.

In some cases, however, ruins are just as attractive to the public as restored or reconstructed sites, and so the remains are left as they are. This also avoids the many issues relating to restoration and reconstruction. For example, archaeologists might have little knowledge concerning how the original structure was assembled or decorated, leading to restored or reconstructed buildings being tainted by an individual's notions of what they would have looked like rather than resembling what they actually looked like. Furthermore, attempts to accurately recreate past structures could violate present-day building and disabled access regulations.

Volunteering opportunities

Even though research and rescue archaeology use similar techniques, volunteering opportunities in rescue archaeology are few and far between – due to the training and experience required to work on building sites, as well as the archaeologists being required to meet tight deadlines (to avoid delaying the development).

It is fortunate, then, that there are ample opportunities for volunteers in research archaeology, where excavations normally take place over a longer period of time (sometimes years) and are led by universities or archaeological societies. Some might be run as community digs (where anyone who is interested can take part) or for the purpose of training archaeology students, although participants are often expected to pay a small fee to cover the costs of training, food and accommodation.

Excavation Supplies

Different archaeological projects have different requirements – depending on where you are in the world, what the field conditions are, and what you're digging up – and all kinds of supplies and equipment could be needed to carry out the excavation work.

The project director normally gives fieldworkers a list of things they should bring in their individual field pack. This can include:

- A WHS, Battiferro, Marshalltown or other archaeological trowel (with the handle painted a bright colour so you can find it if it gets dropped).
- A penknife, butter knife, spatula, spoon, dental pick and sharpened wooden chopsticks (for more delicate digging).
- A small paintbrush.
- Work gloves
- Measuring tape (3 metres).
- A pencil, waterproof pen, or space pen (the latter use pressurised ink, allowing them to write on wet paper).
- A water-resistant notebook.
- Plastic bags (with a zipper-lock).
- A brightly-coloured roll of plastic flagging.
- A compass
- A spirit level

Everything you bring on a dig with you stands a good chance of getting damaged, so it's advisable to take a sturdy (but not brand new) pack. And don't forget to put your names on any tools you buy with a waterproof marker.

*

In addition to tools, you'll also need to bring basic supplies for your general and medical wellbeing (even though all sites will have a trained first aider present). Some basic essentials are:

- A water bottle
- Sun cream
- Bandages
- Antibiotic cream
- Prescription medicines
- Insect repellent
- Bin bags (to put your sodden equipment/clothes in)
- Toilet paper
- Hand sanitiser
- Tweezers
- A torch
- Waterproof matches
- Emergency food

Where you are working will determine what you should wear. A hat, a waterproof poncho, a spare pair of socks, kneepads and work gloves are normally a good starting point, as well as long trousers and sturdy boots when digging (although some digs do not allow the wearing of boots with heavy soles).

Laws, Ethics, and Health and Safety

When preparing an archaeological survey, having permission to dig and knowledge of laws relating to the land are essential.

In addition to legal considerations, it is important to have an open dialogue with the landowner, local residents and *descendant communities* (people whose ancestors lived there) to find out more about the history of the land and how your work will impact them (and vice versa).

Legalities

Different types of land are covered by different types of laws in different countries (with human remains being covered by their own specific legislation), but here are some general rules:

- **Private land:** In most countries you need permission to look (and dig) for artefacts on private land, with the government typically taking control of any sites or artefacts found to protect and promote the heritage of past peoples.
- **Public land:** A permit is normally required to carry out an excavation, and there is often a requirement for the finds to remain in the country for display and further study.
- **Human burials:** These are protected by law on both public and private land, and in almost all countries permission needs to be obtained to disturb them. If human remains are unexpectedly uncovered, therefore, it is important to stop digging and alert the appropriate authorities as well as seeking to determine whether the remains are old or modern. If they turn out to be modern remains, a legal officer such as a medical examiner will

take charge. If they turn out to be old remains, there are still a labyrinth of laws to be navigated – such as reporting their discovery to a state archaeologist, and an obligation to determine the descendants of the human remains.

In the majority of cases human remains are reburied, although under some circumstances they may be excavated.

- **Buried obstacles:** Before carrying out an excavation it is critical that maps are obtained (from companies and government agencies) detailing where utility lines run underground. To disturb them is not just illegal – it's dangerous. Other potential underground hazards to be aware of include the locations of buried toxic waste – able to be found out from government agencies and local residents.

Stakeholders

Archaeologists should always be aware of and considerate to the various *stakeholders* (people interested in or affected by the archaeological work taking place). Stakeholders often have different, conflicting interests, some of which include:

- **Local residents:** Archaeological work is a lot easier if you have the support of the local community. They will know about the history of the land you are working on, can give you advice on the nearest place to grab a bite to eat, and might even lend a hand if your vehicle breaks down.
- **Landowners:** They might not care about archaeology and be unwilling to let you work on their land. Alternatively, they might be interested in your work and be happy for excavation work to take place.

- **Descendants** (or claimed descendants) of the cultural group being excavated.
- **Professional archaeologists** who have previously conducted work on the same sight may agree or disagree with your work, results and interpretations.
- **Amateur archaeologists:** They might be unhappy with other archaeologists working on *their* sites, or enthusiastically offer to show you all the information they have gathered about the site you're working on.
- **Volunteers** who want to get involved.
- **Local historical societies**
- **Looters**
- **Media** (local and national)

Archaeologists should observe *stewardship* (preserving human heritage for the benefit of the collective) and are ethically obliged to share their archaeological findings with the public. The press will often show an interest in your work, and so it is helpful to write a press release to avoid there being any inaccuracies in TV, radio and newspaper reports. And you might also want to invite members of the media for a tour of the site. Although you might not want them to publicize the exact location of the site (which could encourage looting), publicity can be useful to secure the labour of volunteers or advice from experts.

Human remains

Different cultural groups react very differently to the investigation of human remains – with some expressing an eagerness to explore their descendants and others (including many North American indigenous groups) being highly reluctant to disturb the remains of their ancestors in any way at all.[15]

Because of the strong ethical issues surrounding this area of archaeology, most archaeologists avoid disturbing human remains unless absolutely necessary (because they're going to be destroyed by development anyway or because they have extraordinary scientific value).

Laws vary from country to country concerning the discovery of human remains, but in most cases the site director is required to inform the relevant authority (such as a coroner) immediately. If the evidence suggests the burial is ancient rather than more recent, permission may be given for the remains to be excavated; if the evidence suggests the remains are modern, a forensic investigation will probably be required.

In cases where the disruption of graves cannot be avoided, archaeologists may be required to work alongside religious specialists to ensure the remains are excavated and reburied in accordance with the religious rites of the deceased. This can prove to be extremely difficult, seeing as the religious beliefs and practices of the grave's occupants often cannot be determined.

*

When human remains are first found, archaeologists (in addition to taking the necessary legal measures) should consult with members of the local community – explaining the situation and discussing the legally available options with all interested parties. Some archaeologists, who want to avoid ethical controversy at all costs, are highly reluctant to excavate burials, while others highlight the wealth of information bones can provide about past diets, diseases, environments, cultures and daily life.

In the rare instances where the decision is made to excavate human remains, the ongoing work is shielded from the public gaze, and archaeologists might also need to wear protective clothing. This particularly applies to recent human remains, remains buried in lead (which can cause lead poisoning) or airtight coffins (where soft tissue might survive). In addition to protecting the archaeologists, this measure will also prevent them from contaminating material from which DNA might be obtained.

There are various ways in which the human remains might be excavated, including by cutting around and under the remains so they can be excavated in a laboratory. More commonly, the remains are excavated on site, with bones belonging to different parts of the anatomy being placed in separate labelled bags. In addition to this, soil samples will be taken in order to recover smaller artefacts and biological remains, and the burial should be recorded with written and photographic records, including details about the burial practices used (such as orientation, the positioning of different parts of the body, and grave goods) which might be recorded on a pre-printed skeleton diagram.

The entire process of excavating and recording can often be completed by professionals in half a day.

Health and Safety

All tools and equipment used in archaeological work – from large earth-moving machines to hand-held trowels – should be handled with care.

Trowels should be held at a 45 degree angle to the ground and *slice* off soil as opposed to *scraping* it. Failure to do this risks damaging artefacts and features, and obscuring subtle changes in soil colour.

More importantly, handling equipment properly is critical to ensure the safety of fieldworkers. Below are some tips:

- Wear long trousers and sturdy boots to prevent your arms, legs or feet from being injured by shovels.
- Wear a hard hat in deep excavations or when operating heavy machinery.
- Be aware of safety procedures when using heavy machinery.

- Only fill wheelbarrows half-full with soil to prevent injuring your back.
- Any excavation deeper than 4 feet (especially in soft soils) should be shored up to prevent it collapsing on diggers.

In addition to man-made risks, there are plenty of natural hazards you need to be aware of, too:

- **Insect bites and stings:** Use repellent and wear gloves and long sleeves as preventative measures, and seek first aid attention to treat. Ticks can carry fevers such as Lyme disease and burrow their heads into your skin, so make sure you know how to remove them with tweezers.
- **Thorns, nettles and poison ivy:** Once again, make sure you wear long sleeves. A range of products can also be used to treat stings or be applied to your skin in advance as a preventative measure.
- **Wildlife:** Be aware of what animals and plants are found in the project area. Have a guidebook handy to identify insects and an emergency medicine guide to find remedies.

Risk Assessment

Undertaking a formal risk assessment before work begins is critical to ensure the safety of workers, as well as to meet the requirements of insurance policies and health and safety legislation. This includes measures to ensure people are not injured by machinery, subsiding sections and soil heaps, wild animals, overexposure to the sun, amongst many other potential hazards.

Archaeologists often wear high visibility clothing and protective hats and boots, and clear working zones are established for the operation of heavy machinery (with a site supervisor present to prevent anyone entering this area). Sites are also legally obliged to have a first-aid box, a trained first-aider, and for everyone to be aware of what they need to do and where they need to go in the event of an accident.

Survey

Discovering archaeological sites is normally the first stage of fieldwork.

Surveys are carried out in a specific project area, and may focus on sites (known or suspected) from historic sources or aim to test hypotheses about the sorts of places people preferred to live. Despite having walked over almost every inch of the Earth's surface, humans have only chosen certain places to live and conduct various activities. This is normally based on certain characteristics, such as resource availability, and it is important for archaeologists to be aware of these factors in order to conduct a successful survey.

The majority of archaeological work carried out in the present day is surveys. This is partly due to legislation requiring *cultural resources* (archaeological and historic sites) to be examined before planned developments can proceed. In most cases, the survey is merely carried out to find out what's there, but if something particularly important is found the development could be moved and a thorough excavation take place.

Before getting started you need to know why you are conducting the survey, and also seek to find out what's already known about the project area. Material describing archaeological sites can be found in many places, including:

- The internet
- Government offices
- Libraries

Remote sensing and geographic information systems (GIS)

While *remote sensing* is a term used to describe using sophisticated technology to search for sites and objects from afar, a *geographic information system* (GIS) is a computer database containing layers of spatial information which can be used to show where sites might be.

Remote sensing: Instruments used for remote sensing are capable of detecting patterns of buried structures (including roads and walls) and structures concealed by jungle canopies and other vegetation. Essentially, it allows you to see underground without having to dig.

Before using remote sensing, archaeologists study both old and new maps and seek out characteristics (such as a water source) that increase the likelihood of the presence of an archaeological site. These areas are then checked using remote sensing methods, such as:

- **Aerial photography:** has been used since the First World War when pilots flying at low altitudes noticed interesting features in the landscape. Indeed, most remote sensing technology was pioneered by the military need to survey enemy territory.
- **Infrared aerial photography:** is capable of revealing patterns invisible in standard photography. It achieves this by using non-visible parts of the light spectrum.
- **Proton magnetometers:** locate anomalies (especially objects made of metal) by detecting subtle differences in magnetism. They're mainly used to conduct underwater surveys and locate submerged features.
- **Satellite imagery:** is multispectral (capable of seeing things the human eye cannot).

Geographical information systems (GIS): These computerised databases sort and display mapped data. Rather than storing information based on the place name or type of monument, they are *georeferenced* (labelled with coordinates) which enables them to be stored spatially. This information can then be overlaid onto a base map, which allows archaeologists to draw comparisons between past and present landscapes and to easily find things they are interested in (by identifying a specific area on the computerised map and then making selections from the information menu). Admittedly the techniques can be hard to master, but the software and hardware is constantly improving and is a much faster alternative to getting GIS layers by colouring in squares on graph paper overlaid on top of your maps.

Planning the field survey

Now the background work has been completed it is time to plan the field survey.

As well as securing a crew and all the necessary equipment, bear in mind any specific conditions that might be encountered – including the weather, the time of year, the site terrain, and the sorts of finds likely to be discovered. For example, if the site is remote bring plenty of supplies and be aware of where the nearest hospital is, and if your project concerns a wetland site bring sealable containers to keep waterlogged finds wet until they can be stabilised.

The equipment used by survey teams depends on the location and type of survey, but some typical equipment used includes:

- Shovels, trowels and other digging tools.
- Screens (usually quarter-inch mesh) for sifting.
- Coloured flags to mark finds and locations.
- Machetes and root cutters to clear overgrown paths.
- A measuring tape and ruler.
- A compass
- Waterproof pens
- A clipboard and graph paper for drawing maps and finds.
- A magnifying glass for inspecting finds.
- Sealable plastic bags for storing finds.

- A *Munsell colour book*. This has precise numbered coloured chips, which can be matched to soil colours and allow them to be recorded.
- Safety equipment, such as long-sleeved clothing, a hat, a first-aid kit, insect repellent and sun cream.
- Tools to repair equipment and vehicles used on site.

Surface investigation

Conducting a *surface inspection* is the easiest way of finding archaeological sites. In short, it involves driving around in search of ruins or open ground where artefacts are visible on the surface.

You will then need to walk around the site on foot to gather samples of artefacts and ecofacts. Ploughed fields are often go-to places for surface investigations seeing as the turning of the soil unearths artefacts.

Subsurface survey

If vegetation prevents you from seeing anything on the ground surface, you need to dig. And even in instances where artefacts are found on the surface, you'll probably want to find out what else is buried.

The most common subsurface survey method is *shovel testing*, which involves digging a 50 square centimetre hole up to a metre deep (depending on the soil type and project aims). These holes should be large enough to obtain a reasonable sample of artefacts, and to avoid anything being missed the soil is screened – meaning a two-person team (one digging, the other screening) is preferable.

Other, faster methods of subsurface survey can also be used. Some notable mentions are:

- Coring tools and hand-held augers are capable of venturing deeper into the ground than shovel tests. They can be pushed into the ground to pull up soil samples.

- Power augers (normally powered by petrol) can dig down fast to recover samples, but are heavy, expensive and risk churning up the soil and damaging precious artefacts.
- Soil probes typically consist of small-diameter tubes that can be pushed into the ground to recover a soil sample. Their drawbacks include a tendency to get stuck in some soil types and not being able to venture very deep.

When using these faster subsurface survey methods be careful not to let soil from higher levels fall to the bottom of the hole. To do so would risk mixing material from different time periods.

In addition to this, once the subsurface survey has been completed, it is both professional and responsible behaviour to backfill the holes – preventing people or animals from injuring themselves.

Sampling in archaeological survey

The need to take samples arises from the fact that you cannot inspect and shovel test everywhere. Where, how, and what quantity you take in samples depends on the conditions of the survey and its aims.

The *sampling unit* could be an acre or a square mile, or perhaps a *transect* (a line across the project area). The *sample size* (what quantity of units to examine), meanwhile, is decided by a range of factors – including how much time and money the project has, as well as on complicated mathematical equations.

Non-probabilistic or *judgemental sampling* involves searching for archaeological sites based on your knowledge of the area. Some of its principal advantages are:

- It allows lots of sites to be found quickly.
- It reveals information about the area's archaeology.

- It allows data to be collected that can be built upon.

Some of its disadvantages include:

- Sites won't be discovered in unexpected areas.
- The sample is biased and not necessarily representative of the area.
- The quantitative (statistical) study might not be as accurate as it could be.

Probabilistic sampling, on the other hand, uses mathematics to provide a more representative sample. There are three varieties of this type of sampling:

- **Random:** Where each sample unit has the same chance of being selected, removing any bias. To do this, simply assign each sample unit a number and then have your computer choose them at random. Obvious disadvantages of using this method include the possibility of the units clustering in one part of the site and the fact that you're not making the most of your archaeological knowledge.
- **Systematic:** Where sample units are chosen at fixed intervals (e.g. every fifth unit), which ensures good coverage of the entire site. However, it might miss archaeological sites that are aligned using a similar system.
- **Stratified:** Where the site is divided into *strata* (meaningful areas) and a sample is taken from each.

Rather than sticking to one of these sampling strategies, archaeologists will often use a combination of them.

Provenience: is all the potentially useful information about a find and is a critical concept in archaeological work. Some examples of provenience data are:

- The project name.
- The institution funding the project.
- The name and number of the archaeological site (while site names are chosen by the person who records them, in most places an official number is assigned to new sites).
- The name of the person recording the information.
- The names of any other diggers who helped unearth the find.
- The date and time of day it was found.
- A description of the location where it was found.
- An exact map or GPS coordinates of where it was found.

Without this information, your finds are scientifically useless – so make sure you *never* forget to record the provenience of a find! Even if you lose an artefact, you can still study them through the notes, photographs and provenience compiled by the archaeologist who found it.

Cataloguing: Precise records must be kept of the locations of sites and finds. In addition to this, all archaeological material recovered in a project (and their provenience) are recorded in an inventory (called a *field catalogue*), with each bag of materials from each site having their own entries.

Writing up survey findings

It's now time to put all your finds together, and see how they answer your project questions. Processing, interpreting and writing up findings takes much longer than the previous stages of the project, and the finished survey report will include everything you did and found.

The report normally includes things such as:

- The aim and purpose of the survey.

- The survey strategy, techniques and methods, and a justification for why you chose them.
- The project area's environmental background (past and present), including maps and sometimes a GIS database.
- The project area's archaeological and historical background (including sites recorded before your survey).
- The sites visited in the project, as well as everything that was recovered from the sites (including the cultural significance, usefulness for further research and how distributed they were) and what was found out about the sites.
- A summary of what all the information compiled during the survey reveals about the human past in the project area.
- Suggest additional research that can be carried out in the project area to test the hypotheses further and build on the information obtained.

Geophysical survey

Geophysical surveys involve using remote sensing devices linked to computers to reveal what is buried in the ground by detecting differences in the electrical or magnetic properties of features (as long as the soil isn't waterlogged).

Prior to this innovation, archaeologists were limited to *guessing* what lay beneath the soil based on surface sampling and aerial photographs. Now, however, they can establish where to dig far more efficiently, as well as having a good idea of what they are likely to find and what methods should be used.

Equipment used for carrying out geophysical surveys include:

- **Electrical resistance meters:** measure the higher or lower resistance to the flow of electricity using probes. These readings can then be converted into a graphic image on a computer – with black or dark grey areas representing areas of high resistance and white or light grey areas representing areas of low resistance. By interpreting this pattern, it is often possible to see the outlines of features (such as buildings or ditches), although digging is normally required to determine precisely what has caused the pattern. In scientific terms, the only thing *resistivity surveys* reveal are the presence of anomalies underground, and they lack effectiveness in waterlogged soils (because the presence of such a good electrical conductor prevents minor fluctuations in resistance being detected). Nevertheless, resistivity surveys are incredibly useful for locating areas where features are buried, and are particularly effective at locating soil features such as buildings and roads. Therefore, while they are commonly applied on sites that contain the remains of a settled town, they have much less use when investigating a temporary nomadic campsite.
- **Magnetometers:** measure the soil's natural magnetic field, which then allows sensors to be used to detect the presence of alien geology (such as flint and stone) with stronger magnetic fields than the surrounding geology.

In contrast to resistivity surveys, then, magnetometers are far more useful for investigating sites such as temporary prehistoric camps. However, one of its main pitfalls is that large or highly magnetic objects can prevent features with a lower polarity from being detected.

- **Ground-penetrating radar (GPR):** is an expensive piece of kit, and is therefore more commonly used in engineering, oil prospecting and geological surveys than it is in archaeology.

GPR involves sending a radar signal into the ground, which is bounced back to a receiver (at varying strengths and time intervals depending on what is beneath the soil). This can then be converted into data about the condition of the soil and the presence of features.

One of its principal benefits from an archaeological perspective is that it adds a third dimension to the two-dimensional plan obtained by conducting resistivity and magnetometry surveys – revealing the depth of buried features. In sandy soils it is possible to detect and locate small objects with great precision, although its effectiveness is more limited in other subsoil types (such as clay) which are harder to penetrate.

One of the reasons why geophysical surveys are so commonplace in archaeological work today is their non-invasive nature, as well as their promise of surveying large stretches of land faster and more ethically and cost-effectively than through excavation.

The methods used are generally the same, regardless of what equipment you decide to use. Broadly, the geophysical survey process involves:

- Walking backwards and forwards in straight lines (marked out by string) across the site. When using resistivity or magnetometry equipment, a probe (mounted on a frame) is carried by the surveyor and inserted into the ground at regular intervals (approximately 1m) until the entire site has been surveyed. Ground penetrating radar, on the other hand, can be pulled along on wheels and requires slightly less effort on the part of the surveyor.

- The data collected by the equipment includes the global positioning coordinates of where the readings were taken, as well as the data retrieved from beneath the soil which needs to be converted on a computer system. This data will normally appear as a series of dots, grey-scale tones or contour lines.

- The patterns in the data now need to be interpreted to work out what features it is showing. To do this it is important to be aware of the typical shapes and patterns made by certain archaeological sites and features – as well as to combine this data with information obtained through aerial surveys and field walking.

Non-Invasive Archaeology

No matter how much care you take when excavating archaeological material, you're *destroying* it. Once you start digging, the site can never be returned to its original condition and the stratigraphy – a vital way of dating the remains – undermined.

So no, contrary to popular perceptions digging is not the be-all and end-all of archaeological work. Much more time is spent information gathering, which can include a whole range of things – from comparing changes on maps over time, to analysing patterns in the landscape, to studying place names for clues about past uses of sites.

Admittedly in some circumstances the only way to advance our knowledge of a site is by digging, but archaeologists only resort to this if it is deemed absolutely necessary. If there is a means of extracting information from a site without direct interaction, this should be done first.

Most archaeological enquiry, then, usually starts in libraries, records offices and archives – observing photographs and maps for clues – rather than on site with a shovel.

Desktop Analysis

The first stage of information gathering is known as *desktop analysis*. This term distinguishes office-based work from *fieldwork* (research carried out on site).

Some things that are analysed by desktop analysis are reports from previous archaeological projects, archaeological journals, maps, place names and photographs. From this you will be able to determine what is already known about a particular area or site, as well as what questions need to be answered or issues investigated.

Searching for evidence in the field

After desktop analysis has been completed, the next step is to leave the office, head down to your site and observe any evidence on the ground.[16]

It is important to get to know the site better before making a decision about whether or not an excavation is necessary, and this can include both walking across the land with an inquisitive eye and a variety of sophisticated equipment.

More complicated survey techniques include the use of remote sensing instruments (such as GPS resistivity meters, magnetometers and even metal detectors), but there are many simpler techniques that hardly require any equipment at all – such as walking over fields systematically after they have been ploughed and searching for traces of archaeological material that has been brought to the surface.[17]

By walking around a surprisingly large quantity of *above ground archaeology* can often be found, too – ranging from grave stones to rock art to field boundaries – that are already exposed and do not required digging. When conducting a *walkover*, archaeologists should be able to distinguish between natural features in the landscape and those that are the product of human activity. The season, time of day and vegetation all impact on what they can or cannot see (something they should be acutely aware of), and, as well as walking over the landscape for the simple purpose of seeing what's there, they should use the technique in a more systematic manner too. For example, if you find photographs of a site while conducting desktop research, you might want to investigate this further on the ground.

Earthworks (artificial changes in the land level) can also be plotted using electronic distance measurement (EDM) equipment (a method of determining the length between two points using electromagnetic waves). An open field with a clear view of the surrounding landscape is required, as well as three people to operate the equipment.

Using an EDM to conduct earthworks surveys involves the following stages:

- Attach the reflector to a staff (labelled with a vertical scale) and position it where the land rises or falls.
- Make sure the tripod is level using the spirit level.
- Look through the lens at the reflector.
- Use the small knob next to the lens to adjust the focus.
- The EDM will then record the vertical and horizontal scale.
- Record the rise and fall of the landscape by plotting the distance on a graph.

In most cases desktop analysis and searching for evidence in the field complement each other and should not be regarded as separate. Archaeologists will often make visits to the site during their desktop analysis to study and compare their archival findings with visible features on the ground – and the same in reverse. In addition to this, observing the site will normally give rise to new questions and lines of enquiry that need to be researched using maps, photographs, documents and databases.

Field Walking

Before conducting a field walk, it is important to obtain any necessary permits off the government, as well as the consent of the landowner. As well as being legally obliged to do so, succeeding or failing to establish a good relationship with the landowner can make or break a project. For instance, a farmer might be able to tell you where past finds have been uncovered, as well as informing you when they are going to plough. The three or four weeks following the turning of the soil is the best time to look for finds, before the soil becomes compacted again. And some landowners might even possess maps and documents relating to the land, and items they've found themselves over the years.

Broadly speaking, there are two stages to the field walking process. The first stage involves walking systematically across the site to establish where the majority of material is located, before moving onto the second stage where grids are laid out in the more productive areas to investigate them in greater detail.

The first stage can be completed relatively swiftly by using a large number of people walking in lines (marked out by ranging rods) across the site. Depending on how many people there are and the size of the site, these lines might be spaced at anywhere up to 30 metres apart. Spacing them any further apart than this could risk missing small deposits of material, which walkers are supposed to mark using flags or poles.[18] To make it easier to plot the locations of their finds on a map (which have the north at the top), field walking is conducted in a southerly to northerly direction.

In the second stage of field walking, more productive areas of the site are divided into squares (laid out by tape, string and poles) to be examined in more detail. Depending on the size of the site and the number of people involved, these squares can range from as small as 5 x 5m to as large as 20 x 20m (although the aim is to take a sample, not absolutely everything, so larger squares are normally preferred). Each square is assigned a number and plotted onto a base map, before a set amount of time is spent searching for surface finds in each square. It is important to stick strictly to these time limits, because failure to do so could lead to the results being bias in favour of one square over another.

Finds recovered in each square should be sorted into their basic material type (e.g. ceramics, lithics, metals or glass), before being counted and weighed and recorded on the site survey sheet. In most cases the finds themselves are left where they are found (to prevent anything being taken from the site), but sometimes it is necessary to take finds to the laboratory for further examination by an expert. In such instances, the finds are placed in bags labelled with their respective grid reference.

The findings from the squares can be presented in graph form (using graded sized dots) or by colour coding each individual square (reflecting the percentage of each type of artefact found in each grid). By observing these patterns in artefact type and their distribution, archaeologists should then be able to begin identifying where activity was focused on the site, where structures might be located, and what the nature of the buried remains is likely to be.

Metal detectors: often receive bad press in the archaeological field. This includes metal detectorists digging for treasure rather than knowledge, being unwilling to share the location of *their* finds, failing to record contextual evidence, and not seeking permission from the landowner.

Nevertheless, when used in the right way, metal detectors can be useful tools in archaeological work – assisting in the discovery of metal artefacts (especially when walking in a freshly ploughed field) and sites.

Location

The archaeological value of artefacts is dramatically diminished if there is no record of where it was found, and so the precise location of archaeological sites is a critical piece of information. This allows the site to be placed in its larger geographical context, as well as enabling other archaeologists to find the site and conduct further studies in the future.

For these reasons, all surveys begin by determining the precise map location of the site being studied, and specialist surveying skills are required to do this at the necessary level of precision. Fixed points on the Earth's surface have been precisely established (in longitude, latitude and height above sea level) by national mapping agencies (referred to by different names in different countries, including *benchmarks*, *trig points*, *trigonometrical stations* or *triangulation pillars*). Using these points as a starting point, archaeologists can then establish the unknown point they are studying by measuring distances using tape measures or Gunter's chains and measuring variations in height using a theodolite mounted on a tripod.

Today, global positioning systems (GPS) can make life much easier for archaeologists by pinpointing any given location by bouncing radio signals to a series of satellites. The GPS receiver calculates the distance to the satellite by measuring the transmitted signal's travel time and multiplying it by the velocity, and then computes its position and time by making simultaneous measurements to the satellites. Three satellites are required for a 2-dimensional position and a minimum of four satellites are needed to acquire a 3-dimesional position.

GPS devices can range from cheap hand-held devices with a more limited precision to large *total stations* (that are capable of storing vast amounts of data and can have an accuracy of up to 2mm). However, in some areas GPS technology does not function properly (such as places where there is dense rainforest or lots of tall buildings).

Total stations can be used to produce terrain models of sites. The process follows the following steps:

- Set up a base station (and use a satellite to establish its exact position).
- Walk across the site (following flag poles placed in the ground at intervals of 3-5m) while wearing a backpack containing an aerial and transmitter/receiver.

- A three-dimensional record of the walk is stored by the base station, which can then be converted into graphic information on a computer.
- The finished product could be a contoured plan of the archaeological site. If the most sophisticated technology is used, this can be accurate to within 3mm and saves archaeologists from having to spend days on end pacing backwards and forwards across the site and manually plotting their results.

Maps

The importance of maps as an archaeological tool cannot be understated. By showing features such as roads, field boundaries and settlements, they are a useful way of finding out how past peoples interacted with and shaped their environment.

Most of the earliest surviving maps relate to taxation and land tenure. Tithe maps (dating from the Middle Ages to the 19th century) recorded details such as land boundaries, and the names of their owners and tenants, for the purpose of administering the tithe system – whereby the Church received one-tenth of a landowner's income (usually in the form of agricultural produce). Enclosure maps (dating from the 16th to 19th centuries), on the other hand, record the shift from common farming (involving pastureland that anyone could use, as well as large fields divided into narrow strips where different crops were grown) to the division of land into smaller fields bounded by walls or hedges (which were then given to individuals who could prove their right to its ownership).

Such maps offer archaeologists a detailed picture of what the countryside looked like at the time the surveys were completed, and as the Industrial Revolution got underway accurate maps were required in preparation for the construction of turnpikes, canals and railways – for the purpose of acquiring land and ensuring the most efficient cost-effective routes were chosen.

In the United Kingdom, the first mapping agencies were formed in the 18th century. The Ordnance Survey's origins lie in the aftermath of the Jacobite rising of 1745, when the need to map the country arose for the military purpose of countering invasion threats (especially from Napoleon). Its first large-scale map was published in 1801, and it went on to produce maps of England, Scotland, Wales and Ireland – praised for their accuracy and large scale (1:500).

Similar mapping agencies were created in countries across the world during the 20th century – for military purposes in the two World Wars or in order to chart natural resources and natural threats (e.g. fault lines).

Map regression: is a key archaeological technique that involves comparing maps of the same area from different time periods to determine changes to properties, settlements and landscapes or to locate past features.

Patterns in the landscape: don't just reflect natural processes – they reveal past human activity too. Archaeologists who specialise in landscape history are skilled at interpreting patterns in maps to uncover information such as the previous use of land and the development of settlements. Hedge rows and property boundaries often leave discernible patterns behind, as do long abandoned roads, canals and railway lines (with the hedge alignments and property boundaries that still exist preserving their linear character).

Patterns can also be found using topography (e.g. by finding natural features such as springs, there is a high likelihood of finding archaeological sites due to them being regarded as sacred places by past peoples) or by merely being aware of the common characteristics of a particular time or culture (e.g. one technique used to gauge the full extent of the Roman Empire has been searching for signs of their characteristic straight roads and system of land division known as *centuriation*).

<u>Aerial observations</u>

With the assistance of aeroplanes, scaffolding, kites and balloons, archaeologists have been taking aerial photographs for over a century. In its early days the primary motivation was to see large monuments in their wider context, but since then they have become far more varied and complicated with the realisation that aerial views can also be used to detect buried features that are unobservable from ground level – including shadows, and soil and crop marks.

There are a variety of reasons why buried features can be observed from the air in certain conditions. *Soil marks* refer to the contrast in colour between the natural geology and archaeological material that becomes visible after a site is ploughed. The contrast is particularly prominent during the winter and in chalky soils, where features such as burial mounds and ditches often contrast dramatically with the white topsoil.

Other ways of detecting buried features are not as easy to spot as soil marks, and include the effect of the weather and soil depth on vegetation. For example, *parch marks* can reveal the locations of features such as paths and stone walls, because the vegetation growing above them is denied moisture and turns yellow when temperatures rise (although the contrast in colour with surrounding vegetation might only last a few days).

In a similar way *crop marks* can occur as a result of seeds planted over features, such as ditches germinating at a slower rate than those surrounding them (leading to the crops being darker during the few weeks before they ripen). This is also true in reverse – with seeds sown over stony features such as walls taking longer to germinate and being lighter in colour while the crops around them begin to ripen. These subtle differences are best observed in large homogenous crop areas, such as fields of arable crops.

In photography parch marks produce *negative* marks (lighter lines), while crop marks appear as *positive* marks (darker lines). Both types of mark are most abundant from late spring to early autumn (depending on the crop), although the lower sun angle and decline in vegetation during the winter can reveal previously disguised features and subtle variations in contour. The collection of snow and frost in different places and its varying rates of melting, as well as water filling in shallow features on a field can also be used to an archaeologist's advantage during the more inhospitable months of the year.

One final type of mark worth noting are *shadow marks*. These are caused by differences in height on the ground produced by archaeological remains – and are therefore more commonly seen in the context of extant sites rather than previously undiscovered buried ones. The long shadows cast by the higher features are often minor, and you are most likely to spot them when the sun is low in the sky.

It is easy to see, then, why the breakthrough in the form of *aerial observation* has resulted in a vast increase in the number of known archaeological sites.

Types of photographs

Oblique photographs are suitable for recording what can be seen on the ground and are the most common form of monument photograph. It involves using a handheld camera to take photos at a slanting angle to the landscape (either from an aircraft flying at a low altitude or from an elevated location, such as the top of a hill or building).

Vertical photographs, meanwhile, are commonly used to record and map the landscape. They are taken using a plate camera mounted onto an aircraft (using a gyroscope to ensure it stays level), which flies at a fixed altitude. Because the ground is not completely flat alterations have to be made before the features photographed can be superimposed onto a base map. Fortunately for present-day archaeologists, technological progress means much of the *photogrammetry* (the conversion of vertical photographs into accurate scaled plans) is completed by computer programmes and plotting machines.

Although it might sound backwards, black and white film continues to be used in aerial photography due to it being cheap, easy to process and heightening contrasts.

Infrared film is also commonly used for its ability to heighten the contrast in colours (allowing slight variations to be seen more clearly than in regular colour or black and white photography).

Place names

Maps don't just contain drawings – they have writing too. This written element largely consists of place names, which can tell archaeologists a great deal about an area's past uses.

Toponomastics (the study of place names) emerged from the academic discipline of linguistics in the 19th century. Its uses include explaining the origins and meanings of names attributed to settlements, roads, houses, pubs, fields, hills and rivers – essentially *anything* in the human or natural landscape that has a recorded name.

In some parts of the world it's even possible to trace names all the way back to prehistory. The French cities of Rheims, Amiens and Soissons have all retained their pre-Roman names (which derive from the names of their respective Gaulish tribes – the Remi, Ambiani and Suesiones).

'Celtic' Europe (Cornwall, Wales, Ireland, and parts of Scotland, France and Spain) has also been remarkably resilient – a testament to their survival from Roman colonisation. Celtic place names are often composed of two elements – the first being *tre* (roughly meaning 'settlement' or 'hamlet') and the second being the name of the settlement's founder.

One thing place names are particularly good at telling archaeologists is what areas were settled by what groups. For example, many place names in southern England contain Anglo-Saxon elements (who settled there in the aftermath of the collapse of the Roman Empire) such as *wald* ('wood'), *ey* ('island') and *feld* ('field'). Meanwhile, in the northern counties of Yorkshire and Lincolnshire there are an abundance of Viking names (whose Great Heathen Army caused so much trouble for the Anglo-Saxon kingdoms) such as *gate* ('road'), *beck* ('stream'), *tarn* ('lake'), *garth* ('enclosure') and *fell* ('hill').

Excavation Strategies

In archaeology there is no single method of excavation, with strategies varying depending on a range of factors – including the type of site, and whether the dig is research or rescue archaeology.

Below are some common methods used by archaeologists:

- **Preserving archaeology *in situ* (PARIS):** involves trying to preserve as much of the archaeological material as possible, in the place and condition it was originally found (hinted at in the Latin words *in situ* – meaning 'in place' or 'not removed'). Unfortunately, it is rarely possible to leave all the archaeological material untouched. Instead, a compromise is often struck where a small portion of the site is excavated using *keyhole archaeology*.
- **Keyhole archaeology:** one example of keyhole archaeology is called a *watching brief*. These are carried out during rescue archaeology projects, when engineers drill into the soil or dig foundation trenches to see if any archaeological material is uncovered. If archaeological material is found, then construction work might be stopped to allow a more sophisticated excavation to take place. However, in reality it is incredibly difficult to interpret the odd jumble of finds that might be pulled out of the ground by the digger, and has the additional drawbacks of risking damaging archaeological remains and being much less precise than work carried out by experienced archaeologists with hand-held tools.
- **Test pits and trial trenches:** are also used in rescue archaeology, and can be sunk into the ground in areas where construction work is planned to take place.

Although preferable to keyhole archaeology, they are still small-scale excavations (heightening the risk of significant archaeological remains being missed) and normally raise more questions than they answer. However, they can be useful for assessing the nature and extent of archaeological remains at a site, as well as guiding judgements about whether a full scale excavation is necessary.

- **Research excavations:** have more freedom in terms of time and methods than rescue archaeology. The position of trenches can be based upon the nature of the site and research questions rather than on where engineers are placing shafts, piles or trenches for service pipes.
- **Total archaeology:** large-scale excavations are the most extreme and expensive digs. For this reason they are relatively rare, and are normally funded by government agencies or utility companies as a part of a wider objective – e.g. new transport infrastructure or mineral extraction. These complement small-scale excavations (which provide in-depth information concerning a specific site), by putting the information into a wider context and revealing patterns across an entire landscape.

While *keyhole archaeology* and *total excavation* represent the extremes of archaeological digging, most excavations lie somewhere in between.

How to set up a research project

Although the process will vary from project to project, here is a typical approach to setting up a research project...

Excavations are normally headed by a *director*. In research archaeology, the director's first job is to obtain permission to dig. As well as obtaining permission off the landowner, they also need to convince the relevant government authorities that the excavation is necessary – e.g. because it is the only means of answering a specific research question, or because the site is threatened with being destroyed by development.

The finished product of this first stage is a *project design*. This is a document stating what is known about the site being studied, why excavation is necessary, and how the work will enhance our knowledge of the past.

At the same time, it is also important to ensure sufficient funding has been secured to cover the entire project's expenses. Funding might come from academic institutions, or a mixture of small grants from individual donors, charities or archaeological societies.

Directors are also responsible for a range of mundane tasks that are essential to the smooth-running of any dig.

Deciding when the dig takes place is often dependant on when volunteers are available. As many volunteers are students, lots of digs take place during university holidays.

Other decisions include the excavation's length, how many people are required, what skill levels the diggers need to be at, and how much volunteers will be charged for food and accommodation.[19]

Once the issues of permits, finances and staffing have been resolved, the director needs to acquire the necessary tools and equipment for the dig.

Even basic small-scale excavations can require a long list of equipment. A range of tools and supplies are needed to dig, mark out trenches, move excavated soil, sift soil and store finds.

Most the tools used are not designed specifically for archaeology – but trowels are one notable exception. Curved gardening trowels are unsuitable for use in archaeological excavations (as they have a tendency to dig holes), and in the United Kingdom the most popular trowel used by archaeologists is the WHS. Made by Spear & Jackson, it has a 10cm steel blade and a rubber handle and finger guard. Other popular archaeological trowels include the slightly shorter and broader Italian-made Battiferro pointing trowel (in continental Europe) and the slightly longer 11.4cm Marshalltown pointing trowel (in North America). Trowels are the most important part of an archaeologist's kit and have many uses – as a scraper, lever or blade. On the most delicate sites, they might also be the only 'large' tools allowed.

Here are some other basic tools needed for excavations:

- Shovels (with long handles to prevent backache). Round and pointed ones are best for backfilling, and square-bladed ones are best for skimming floors and walls as well as for chopping roots.
- Hand tools for finer digging, including trowels, spoons, knives, spatulas, dental picks, sharpened chopsticks and fine brushes.
- Dustpans, buckets and wheelbarrows for removing soil.
- Screens for sieving (with varying mesh sizes depending on the type of soil and expected finds). If you're water screening as well as dry screening a water pump will be required (containing a connector system that divides pipes and hoses to go to different screens).
- String and sturdy poles to set out excavation units.
- Brightly coloured flagging to mark the location of finds.
- Plastic sheeting to protect excavations from rain and dust.
- Resealable plastic bags for finds.
- Large heavy-duty plastic bags for soil samples.
- A compass

- Line levels and plumb bobs (used for accurately measuring the locations of features).
- Long (30-50m) and short (3m) measuring tapes.
- A clipboard, ruler, protractor, graph paper, field notebook (with waterproof paper), and waterproof pens and pencils.
- Field forms (used for recording specific information).
- Cameras (in waterproof cases).
- Machetes, hatchets, chainsaws and weed whips for removing vegetation.
- Basic tools for fixing equipment.
- Locks and chains for securing equipment.
- Water and food.
- Ice (for emergencies).
- First aid kit (containing the phone number for and directions to the nearest hospital).

In some cases it is impractical to use only hand-held tools to excavate. If test pits or trial trenches find nothing of archaeological value in the topsoil, this can be cleared far more efficiently using a back hoe or scraper bucket (without teeth). Admittedly, this does incur an extra cost, raise health and safety concerns, and risk damaging archaeological remains, but is often deemed necessary when weighed against the vast amount of time it can save.

Here is some large-scale equipment often used in excavations:

- **Front-end loaders** can scrape off soil, pick it up, or push it to one side with its wide open bucket.
- **Backhoes** can dig deep at speed with their narrow bucket (allowing archaeologists to get an idea of how deep the site's cultural deposits venture).
- **Scraper pans** can cut thin slices of soil, and dispose of it elsewhere.

- **Hydraulic elevators** have an arm that allows them to be positioned to one side and dig without disturbing the cultural deposits.
- **Draglines** also sit to one side, but have a much larger arm that can remove lots of soil. However, it is not useful for large sites due to its treads having a tendency to tear up soil.

- **Hydraulic coring machines** (used for collecting deep samples).

- **Portable cabins** for storing equipment securely.
- **Flotation equipment**
- **A cover** to protect the excavation from sun, rain and dust.

In addition to this, a wide variety of tools can be used to map the site. This can range from using compasses, tape measures and graph paper to sketch scaled drawings by hand, to using more sophisticated equipment such as:

- **A transit:** is set up at the site's *datum point* (the point from which everything will be measured) and are essentially composed of a telescope, a large compass and a tripod. The fieldworker then looks through the scope at the *stadia* (measuring) rod and takes a note of the reading, as well as the *compass* (horizontal) and *scope* (vertical) angles. From this you should then be able to calculate the distance, direction and elevation of specific points on the site (including excavation units and features), and plot them on paper to create a two-dimensional map.
- **Total stations:** are set on a tripod and use a laser from an *electronic distance measuring device* (EDM) to

measure the distance, direction and elevation of points on a site. The laser is detected by a prism target (as opposed to a stadia rod), which is placed on the feature being mapped. The signal bounces off the target and returns to the Total Station, which calculates the distance and angle of the object. Although these can be heavy, expensive and complicated to operate, they have many advantages. They are fast, accurate, does not entail having to clear thick vegetation to see the rod (as is the case with a transit), and if you connect the data-logger to a computer it will draw the map for you.

- **Plane tables:** allow you to create a map in the field rather than having to take your measurements back to the lab.
- **Spatial technology** (including *photogrammetry* and *3-D laser scanning*): can create three-dimensional images by taking photographs from different angles or using a laser to scan zillions of points (revealing things that are hard to see with the naked eye). It is frequently used to create more specialised maps (such as buildings and other standing monuments), although the kit can be expensive and hard to use.

When mapping, don't forget to bring radios (so the person operating the instrument can communicate with the person holding the rod or laser target) and a plastic cover to protect the instrument from rain.

The Archaeological Dig

Archaeological excavation involves digging, recording and interpreting the physical remains of past people who lived in an area in order to better understand their culture.

It is very difficult to predict how much you will need to dig to find answers to your research questions. Progress can be slower or faster based on the weather, quantity of finds, soil type, site location and expertise of the diggers; and the amount you are able to dig is often determined by the amount of labour you have at your disposal.

Mapping

Because you need to know the precise location of everything you find, the first stage of an excavation is to map the site.

To do this you need to establish a datum point (from which everything will be measured with your mapping instrument). This point can be on the edge or at the centre of the site, but it is most commonly placed outside the site's southwest corner. If this established trend is followed, all points are mapped in terms of their distance north and east from the datum point. The datum point itself also needs to be mapped in relation to an official marker (e.g. a point on a published map or a government survey marker) with a precise known location. It should also be located somewhere that is unlikely to be excavated and in a place that gives an uninterrupted view of the whole site (to allow optical measuring instruments to be used or tape measures to be run from it). On hilly sites, therefore, several datum points might be required, with each one overlooking a specific area of the site.

The datum point might be marked by an existing feature in the landscape, such as a gatepost, or you might make your own by hammering a post into the ground.

A grid covering the entire site is then set up using stakes and string. Each excavation unit is named in terms of the grid lines, and a corner of the unit is selected to be the *unit datum*.

Positioning excavation units

Excavation units are positioned based on what you already know or want to find out. For instance, if remote sensing detects anomalies beneath the surface, you'll probably want to dig there to find out if there's any archaeological material.

On shallow sites large block units can be opened (measuring a number of metres), and wide units should also be maintained on sites with deeper deposits in case the walls cave in.

As described in the 'Survey' chapter, excavation units can be situated based on your own knowledge of the site (a *judgemental sample*) or on *random* or *systematic sampling* (once the site has been divided into meaningful sections, such as domestic, agricultural and ceremonial areas).

Digging will normally continue until *culturally sterile* soils are reached (where there are no longer any signs of human activity). In order to avoid missing anything (because many structures are constructed over older structures), it is important to keep excavating until you reach the natural surface that the first occupants of a site walked on.

Even in the non-existent scenario of having unlimited resources at your disposal, archaeological sites are rarely fully excavated. As well as taking financial constraints into consideration it is important to save some remains for future generations (when better technology might allow new types of information to be obtained from the site).

Removing the topsoil

On some sites undisturbed archaeological material can be found on the surface, so serious excavation work can begin right away. In most cases, however, vegetation and topsoil disturbed by natural or human activity (such as root growth, burrowing or ploughing) needs to be removed first.

The way in which the topsoil is removed depends on the scale of the excavation and the nature of the site – with hand-held tools such as spades and pickaxes being used on small-scale excavations and machinery being used on larger ones. Great care must be taken throughout the process and the archaeologist in charge of the stripping of the topsoil needs to have a sound knowledge of the local soils and geology so they can tell the difference between disturbed soil, natural features and archaeologically significant material. Metal detectors can be used to see if there are any metal objects hidden in the soil, and it's better to take off too little topsoil than to dig too far and risk damaging features and artefacts.

The site is then cleaned (to reveal undisturbed archaeological features) and planned before any decision is made about where to excavate. Cleaning uses a range of tools such as a trowel, a hoe and a dustpan and brush, and is best done when the soil is dry to avoid it smearing and obscuring the edges of features. Very specific techniques are used when cleaning soil off archaeological material to prevent causing damage, including using a brush to *flick* soil off the surface of the feature rather than *dragging* the soil across it.

Any waste material (also known as *spoil*) from the cleaning process is discarded on a spoil heap. These heaps are positioned away from areas that might need excavating (to prevent the spoil from spilling into excavation units), but not so far away that diggers have to walk long distances. Different parts of the site might have their own spoil heap, and there are often three kinds of heaps – one for turf to backfill the site at the end of the excavation, one for topsoil (fertile soil that farmers use to plant their crops in), and one for less fertile subsoil.

Initial site plan

Before digging can begin, it is important to produce a detailed plan of the site to document its original condition – including any features that have been revealed by the cleaning process. You must also keep an accurate drawn and photographic record of the site (i.e. anything you're about to destroy) throughout the excavation.

The plan should be two-dimensional, and is produced by using graph paper and the site grids as a guide – with the lines on the graph paper corresponding with lines laid out on the site grid.

Make sure you have both a long tape measure (30-50m) and a short one (3m), as well as a drawing grid for drawing smaller details (consisting of a 1m x 1m frame, divided into 100mm squares by string or wire). The grid is then placed on top of the feature(s) you want to draw. Making sure the squares on the grid correspond with the squares on your graph paper, you can then trace the outlines of the features onto some tracing paper (using the graph paper underneath as a guide).

Before producing these more detailed drawings, however, you should use the site grid to draw the outlines of the most prominent features. To do this, attach a long tape measure to two pegs on opposite sides of the site and mark the precise points where the tape measure intersects the edges of the feature on your tracing paper. To ensure accuracy, you should stand directly over the point being measured and look down at the tape measure. Depending on the shape and complexity of the feature, other measurements of the feature may also have to be taken with a shorter tape measure before it is sketched.

The finished product of this repetitive process will be a two-dimensional plan illustrating the outlines of the main features that can be seen before the excavation work begins. You will also need to write a unique reference number next to each feature on the plan, as well as the height of the top of the feature above sea level.

Phasing, and digging levels and strata

Phasing and *stratigraphy* are the principal archaeological tools for understanding phases of past human activity on a given site.

Phasing involves asking questions such as: Do these features belong to the same period of activity, and if not can they be arranged into chronological order? Are the different periods of activity evolutionary and linked to each other, or were there periods of use and abandonment?

In order to answer these questions, you must investigate the different layers in the site's soil, known in geological terms as its *stratigraphy*. This is founded on the basic premise that the lowest archaeological deposits on a site are the oldest and the highest deposits are the newest. Because of this, excavations involve examining and removing archaeological material in turn, starting with the most recent deposits, and continuing until you reach the natural geological surface.

Excavation takes place at a slow pace to ensure nothing is missed. It is important to pay constant attention to the soil's layering – removing one layer at a time and numbering them sequentially.

While the term *soil stratum* refers to layers already in the ground, *levels* are layers designated by archaeologists.

Some examples of layers include:

- **Natural strata:** are layers of soil that formed naturally and can be told apart based on their colour, texture or contents.

- **Cultural strata:** are layers of soil that contain different cultural material intermixed with the natural stratum.
- **Arbitrary levels:** are used when it is hard to see where the soil layers begin and end. They should have a uniform depth and be correlated to the natural and cultural strata once the layers have been exposed in the unit walls.

Some sites use a combination of these methods – and don't forget, you should never mix materials from different strata or levels.

When you reach the end of a strata or level, it is essential that you stop digging in order to map, photograph and describe the soil colouring and any artefacts or features on the unit floor. You will also need to decide what the relationship is between the two deposits. The simplest relationship is where the second deposit is covered by the first, and other possibilities include the deposits surrounding, abutting or cutting through each other.

It is not always easy reaching the oldest deposit. Sometimes you'll encounter obstacles such as box culverts (a stone water channel). If this happens, you must assign the box culvert a context number, clean it, draw and photograph it, and record its precise location before dismantling it. Then you will be able to continue excavating below the box culvert until no further finds are found and the site supervisor is convinced the natural geological surface has been reached.

Stratigraphic analysis becomes even more complex when deposits do not merely lie on top of each other. In urban areas that have been occupied for hundreds or thousands of years, it is not uncommon to encounter an extremely complex mixture of deposits – abutting, surrounding or cutting through others. This is the product of successive generations adapting structures built by previous generations or constructing new buildings on top of old ones.

Digging a section

Once the site has been cleaned and planned, archaeologists might choose to dig *sections* through some of the exposed features to investigate their stratigraphy and contents before the main excavation gets underway.

Digging a section involves cutting a vertical incision through a feature, which allows you to examine their contents and the various colours and textures of soil that fill the feature. From this you might be able to get a general understanding of past human activity at the site, and when it happened.

Before getting started, the area where you're going to dig the section needs to be cleaned again, before marking out both ends of where you're going to excavate with nails and string. The excavation should be a reasonable size (around 2m), but not so big that it involves more work without yielding extra information about the nature of the site.

Before digging, make sure you take photographs of the feature, including a scale (normally a pole or rod of 0.5m or 1m, marked at 100mm intervals). Each photograph will then be stored in a register, and a unique number will be assigned for all the data recovered from that area of the site.

Next, the soil is removed from the feature layer-by-layer, with finds from each layer being recorded.

Choosing where to dig a section is no easy task, and you will often happen across several features within the feature you're digging a section through. Should this happen, you will need to plan and section each of these features individually. The end goal is to ensure all the features are recorded in three dimensions, with the section dig revealing the depth of each layer (in contrast to plan records, which reveal how far each layer extends horizontally).

Shovelling and trowelling

Typically fieldworkers will begin an excavation with shovels and switch to smaller tools once finds begin to emerge. Trowels are used near the bottom of a strata or level to give the cleanest possible unit floor. Even smaller tools – such as brushes, chopsticks and dental picks – are used when artefacts and features are exposed to avoid causing any damage.

When digging, start at one end of the ditch and loosen soil by pulling the pointed heel of the trowel towards yourself with a scraping motion. You should start to cut a small trench, proceeding gradually and carefully until you have a better idea of what the fill is like.

In order to avoid venturing too deep and penetrating a new layer, it is a sensible precaution to progress in *spits*. This involves removing approximately 30mm to 50mm of soil in a small area at one end of the trench, and doing the same across the rest of it if no change in the soil's texture or colouration is identified. The process is then repeated until you reach a new layer. It cannot be overestimated how important it is to excavate horizontally rather than digging holes, and because of this flat archaeological trowels should be used rather than gardening ones (with the former being better suited to removing soil in flat, horizontal movements that expose finds rather than scooping them out).

Once the object has been exposed it needs to be measured, drawn and photographed *in situ* (Latin for 'in place') before it is removed from the ground and loses its context. In the majority of sites, finds are so abundant that it is impractical to do this for every archaeological deposit, and so smaller finds are normally unearthed through screening or flotation.

Unit floors should be cleaned using a trowel to allow precise measurements and to reveal features. Some common features are:

- Clusters of artefacts or bones.
- Obvious marks left by humans, such as walls or graves.

- *Postmolds* (circular soil stains left by the posts of structures). The stains result from the posts decaying where they originally stood or from the posts being removed and the holes filling with vegetation and decaying.

- Dark stains (circular or oblong) in the soil marking the remains of garbage or storage pits. Larger stains might reveal the floors of man-made structures.
- Hearths and fire pits showing signs of burning.

While some features are small enough to be removed, larger features (such as walls) might not even be partially removable. In order to investigate these larger features in more detail, you might need to adjust the placement of your excavation units so more of it can be revealed.

Contexts

In order to be as scientific and objective as possible during an excavation most archaeologists avoid applying descriptive terms such as 'feature', 'ditch', 'layer' or 'soil' to archaeological finds. Instead, they strive to use neutral terms (called *contexts*), which saves them from having to re-write their notes every time a feature that was initially described as one thing is later reclassified as something else. Judgement should be saved until the data gathering is complete and the project has entered the post-excavation analysis phase.[20]

Each context is assigned a unique *site code* (alternatively known as an identification number) when they are excavated.

Measuring

Before removing any artefact or feature, it is essential that you measure their exact position in three dimensions. If the datum point is placed in the customary position (outside the southwest corner of the site), the artefact or feature's distance from it can be measured in one of two ways: the distances north and east from the datum point or the angle and distance from the datum point. To measure the depth of an artefact or feature use a piece of string tied to the datum corner stake at surface-level. Hold the string over the find (using a small line level hanging on the string to keep it level) and measure the depth from the string.

Screening and flotation

If a site is likely to yield small finds that are hard to spot while digging, excavated soil is screened for archaeological material before being discarded.

Screens can have different sizes of mesh depending on the type of soil, but the standard size is a quarter inch.

There are two types of screening – *dry screening* and *water screening*.

Dry screening is easier to set up, but can be hard work because you have to shake it and remove unwanted material. Water screening, on the other hand, requires a water source and taking the time to set up a pump, hoses and waterscreen station. Its main advantage is that it allows you to use finer mesh sizes and in turn recover much smaller objects, as well as the water heightening contrasts in colour which makes archaeological material easier to spot.

Soil flotation, meanwhile, involves using water and fine screens to recover very small archaeological remains. It works on the principle that the remains are less dense than water, so they will float on the water's surface rather than sinking to the bottom.

As a rough guide, take a 300 x 300 x 100mm sample from each strata or level in each unit for flotation. These samples should be removed with a shovel or trowel in large solid chunks to prevent the fragile remains it might contain from being damaged. Additional soil samples might also be taken to save for future studies.

Flotation tanks assume a variety of forms. Some are very basic, others are more complex, but they have a number of things in common. A mesh screen is put on top of a water tank. Soil is then tipped onto the mesh and the tank is gradually filled with water – slowly enough to allow the soil to break down and release any archaeological material it might contain. Lighter items will pass out via a spillway near the top of the tank, and are referred to as the *light fraction*. The water that spills over the top of the tank is then passed through a series of screens of varying mesh sizes, which trap larger material called the *heavy fraction*.[21]

All the material recovered from screening or flotation is left to dry out before being sorted, bagged and labelled (or, in the case of waterlogged finds, placed in jars and submerged in water).

If lumps of soil resist being broken down, soak them in hydrogen peroxide prior to subjecting them to screening or flotation.[22]

Finds in context

Material recovered from each deposit or context during an excavation is placed in its own *finds tray*. This is normally a plastic tray with a waterproof label on which the site code and context number is written in waterproof ink. Each time a deposit is encountered, the digger will be provided with a new tray to keep material recovered from different layers separate.

Depending on the nature of the site, some finds might be classified as *special*. This could include finds that can be dated in absolute or relative terms, or finds that provide vital information that can be used to interpret the site (such as the layout and contents of graves). Such finds are recorded and described in much greater detail than routine finds – being assigned a unique number, having its precise location recorded in three dimensions (using a theodolite and a tape measure or EDM equipment), and its details written on the context recording sheet and special finds register.

Sampling strategy

The sampling strategy (the types and quantities of archaeological material kept from the excavation) is decided by the site director and site supervisors based on the kind of site they're working on.

In the case of ecofacts, certain types of finds are more likely to have been preserved in different site conditions. Organic remains are far less likely to survive in acidic soils than in neutral or alkaline ones, and their best chance of preservation is in a waterlogged environment. Deposits that are charred, on the other hand, (such as hearths) destroy the remains of things such as insects, plants and pollen, but are favourable to the preservation charred plant remains and charcoal.

There are numerous varieties of sample, with *bulk* and *column sampling* being those most commonly carried out by volunteers and *monolith* and *Kubiena sampling* being reserved for professional archaeologists.

Single context samples

In column sampling, samples are taken from a series of related deposits, but the most common sampling method is *single context sampling*. This is pretty much what it says on the tin – material extracted from a single context. However, you must take care to ensure the sample is representative of the context and is not contaminated by material from other layers.

The quantity of material taken as a sample from a context depends on various factors, including if there are facilities on site to determine if the samples contain biological remains. If the answer to this is yes, an initial 10 litre sample might be processed, followed by a further 30 litres if the test comes back positive. If the answer is no, a 40 litre sample might be taken to an off-site laboratory, where the first 10 litres will be analysed, followed by the rest if the results are promising.

A sample register and sample recording sheets are used to record samples, and include information such as where it was taken from, why it was taken, what it might reveal about an individual feature or the site as a whole, what percentage of the entire deposit the sample represents, and whether it's been taken from an occupational deposit (potentially containing evidence of past human activity) or an environmental deposit (potentially containing evidence about a site's past environment).

A waterproof label should also be taped to the bag or container holding the sample (with the date, site code, trench code, context number, sample number and type of sample written on it) and an identical one should be placed inside.

Bulk samples

Bulk soil samples can be taken using various methods. One example is where a vertical column of material is sampled to keep the stratigraphy intact. Others entail taking samples from each individual layer in order to analyse their relationship to each other. Although they cannot be used on all features (with deep sections being preferred), both of these methods allow archaeologists to study how the site has changed over time – whether it is defined by continuity, or gradual or sudden change.

There are two possible ways of obtaining samples in this way:

- **The columnar method:** is where a trowel is used to cut accurately-measured blocks of sediment from a deposit (measuring 250mm x 250mm x 60mm, although the thickness may vary). This produces a series of samples whose relationship with neighbouring deposits is recorded but not preserved.
- **Kubiena and monolith-type boxes:** are essentially metal tins (measuring approximately 500mm x 140mm x 100 mm) which can collect a block of soil without disturbing its structure. Composed of brass, zinc or tin, they are pushed or hammered into the section. When sampling deep sections, multiple tins will be required. The tins should be numbered and overlap each other by approximately 50mm to prevent there being any gaps in the column sample. This method is easiest when used in soft soils, which allows the samples to be cut out, rather than being dug out with a sharp spade. The tins should be wrapped tightly to ensure the sample remains intact, as well as being labelled upon removal.

Site matrix

Once a ditch has been fully excavated, you should attempt to place it in the wider context of the site – showing how it can be related to other excavated features. This is no easy task, seeing as it often relies on an individual's judgement and interpretation, which are often revised multiple times as more and more evidence is produced by the excavation.

In 1973, while working on excavations in the English city of Winchester, the archaeologist Edward Harris devised the *Harris matrix* to illustrate relationships in stratigraphy.

In simple terms, the Harris matrix is a seriation diagram which has the appearance of a family tree (with the minor exception of the boxes containing context numbers rather than names). The uppermost context in the diagram represents the most recent deposit, and different shaped boxes are used to distinguish between different types of features. In the simplest ditches, the diagram will have a linear structure with one context lying over another. If features are found within features, however, they will be represented with a separate branch off the main tree.

Once a ditch's individual matrix has been completed, its wider context needs to be established by connecting it to a matrix of the entire site. This can only be achieved if part of the ditch cuts through (or is cut by) another feature, allowing a relationship to be drawn between the two. Unfortunately, it is not always possible to find clear physical relationships between contexts.

Processing finds on site

Finds extracted from archaeological sites are initially taken to a field laboratory or finds shed, where they are cleaned, inspected, catalogued and stored. Sometimes emergency conservation treatment is required, although the majority of the work is mundane and repetitive.

Each digger will have a finds tray (labelled with the site code and context number) which they bring to the field laboratory at the end of each day (or if the tray is full).

When sorting and cleaning these finds, you should be aware that the process could destroy critical evidence, including blood stains, paint, fabric and food residues. Prior to doing this, then, the site director will consult with the finds supervisor to decide what material can be washed, as well as what to keep or discard. The decision will hinge on a range of factors, such as the type of site and finds, and what information they are likely to produce.

At the beginning of each day, a volunteer will line up the finds trays from the previous day's digging for the site director and supervisors to review.[23] The supervisors will often have different areas of expertise and will look for patterns or anomalies amongst the finds.

After this, the volunteer can sort the finds into different materials. Stronger finds can be placed in robust paper bags (with small holes to allow moisture to escape) based on their context and type. The site code, trench number and context number are all written on the bag using a waterproof marker, and a label containing the same details is placed inside the bag. Each bag is then typically placed into a large plastic box with all the other finds recovered from the same trench (making sure larger, sturdier finds are stored at the bottom of the box and smaller, more fragile ones at the top).

Due to the high cost of storing and studying large quantities of finds, when considering how many *common* or *bulk finds* to keep a balance has to be struck between the information they're likely to produce and the investment in time, labour and money. Therefore, the site director will normally keep only a sample of the common finds that are most likely to have a significant impact on interpreting and understanding the site's past.

Before discarding the rest of the common finds, they are washed and left out to dry just in case the dirt was concealing any details that could elevate them to a higher level of importance. If not, they are counted, weighed and described, before being buried on part of the site where they're unlikely to be disturbed. The location of the discarded material should then be recorded in case future researchers have a need for it.

Fragile finds

While many finds – such as those made from brick or stone – do not require special attention, some, more delicate ones require immediate treatment. As soon as these more delicate finds are taken out of the ground, the dramatic change in environment can undermine their stable condition – with factors such as sunlight, air and physical handling causing rapid deterioration.[24] The speed of deterioration will depend on what the find is composed of, as well as how significant the difference is between their buried environment and the one to which they are now exposed. Materials being recovered from wet environments are amongst the worst affected and it is essential that you try to replicate their buried condition as quickly as possible.

In the case of most metals, damp conditions can cause them to decay and therefore they should be left to dry for 24 hours. Once they are dry, these finds can then be placed on top of screwed-up acid-free tissue paper inside a rigid polystyrene box (to prevent them breaking if they turn out to be brittle). A relative humidity indicator card (containing a coloured scale that reacts to damp conditions) and silica gel bags (of a similar weight to the find) should also be placed inside the box. In order to ensure the humidity remains below the required 15%, the box then needs to be sealed tightly, checked frequently, and the silica gel replaced whenever necessary.

Two notable exceptions of this rule for metals are solid silver and gold, both of which are stable. However, in most cases these metals have been added as thin layers on top of other materials, and are therefore likely to be fragile too.

In addition to this, if metal objects are uncovered with organic material attached to them, they should be treated in the same way as waterlogged finds and specific conservation advice sought as soon as possible. Waterlogged finds should be kept in a sealed box filled with distilled water, preferably stored in a refrigerator.

Biological finds

Natural material can reveal all sorts of information about a site that you might not be able to obtain from artefacts and features. Things such as shells, plant remains and pollen can provide vital clues concerning what the environment was like at the site in the past. For example, the quantity and type of pollen found at a site can reveal how much vegetation was present in the past environment, what it was surrounded by – be it grassland, woodland or wetland – and whether or not coppicing had taken place. Similarly, the presence of certain insect remains can indicate whether conditions on the site were dry or wet, or wild or cultivated based on their habitat requirements.

Other environmental finds, such as bones, insects and food remains, can give archaeologists an insight into how past people exploited the site – what crops were grown, what animals were domesticated and reared, and the scale of farming, as well as what people were eating and what diseases they might have suffered from. It might also be possible to carbon date some organic materials, including plant remains and wood, to estimate how old certain parts of the site are.

Finishing a dig

If you're returning to the site for future excavations, excavation units can be covered and fenced off. If not, you should backfill the excavated units and remove any stakes left in the ground. To help future archaeologists, you might also leave markers (such as plastic sheeting) at the bottom of the units to show where you dug.

Record-keeping

If you fail to keep detailed records of your excavation and finds, you are essentially guilty of looting. By missing or losing information as a result of careless procedures, it could be lost forever and jeopardise your chances of understanding the site. Even unexciting finds should be recorded and published so future researchers can perhaps interpret finds the current excavators do not yet understand.

Each archaeological artefact or feature is given a unique context number as it is excavated. The number is allocated sequentially from the context catalogue. For example, the top layer of trench 4 might be numbered 400, with the next layer in the trench being number 401, the layer after that 402, and so on. The name of the trench and its grid references and context number are written at the top of the recording sheet. The remainder of the sheet is used to record details about the deposit's physical appearance. However, instead of allowing the digger to use their subjective judgement and write what they want, there are a number of tick boxes on the sheet for recording key characteristics.

Differences in soil colour can be best distinguished when it is damp, and in some instances it is acceptable to give dry soil a little spray. Because soil is rarely one easy-to-define colour, archaeologists normally describe it in terms of its predominant shade, such as blackish, orangey or whitish. In addition to this, as the excavation proceeds the digger will need to take notes of how easy it is to distinguish between layers. This is known as *horizontal clarity* and can be classified as good, medium or poor.

The composition of soils, meanwhile, are determined by the size of their particles:

- The finest soils are clay and silt.
- Middling soils are sand and gravel, whose particles are sized 2mm and 2-4mm respectively.
- Large soils are pebbles (4-60mm), cobbles (60-250mm) and boulders (more than 250mm).

Unfortunately, soils often do not have a consistent composition and require more elaborate descriptions that combine multiple soil types, such as silty gravel (a silty deposit with some gravel) or gravelly silt (vice versa).

The strength of the soil deposit when placed under stress (also known as *compaction*) is gauged in different ways depending on the soil type. For finer deposits, you should attempt to mould a moist sample with your fingers – with samples being classified as *friable* if they crumble, *soft* if they are easily mouldable, *firm* if they are mouldable when pressure is applied, and *hard* if they resist moulding. Soils with larger particles, on the other hand, are classified as *loose* if they easily crumble, *firm* if they maintain their form when pressure is applied, and *compact* if they cannot be broken.

Any other material found within a layer (ranging from natural materials such as shells to materials from human activity such as pottery) are referred to as *inclusions* and are documented in terms of their size (smears, flecks, and small, medium or large inclusions) as well as their frequency (rare 1-3%, sparse 3-7%, moderate 10-20%, common 20-30%, very common 30-40% and abundant 40-50%).

*

Context recording sheets differ depending on who you're working for, but they all record the same essential information about a context, including:[25]

- The context number.
- The deposit's character, including size and colour.
- The deposit's relationship to other contexts.
- Your interpretation of the deposit.
- Reference numbers of any finds, soil samples, drawings and photographs from the context.

The most important information of all is the *provenience* of a find – or, to use plain English, where it came from. The 'Survey' chapter includes some of the information you need to record a find's provenience during the survey phase, but in the excavation phase even more information is required. Some of this additional information includes:

- The exact three-dimensional location coordinates of the find.
- What excavation unit and strata or level it was found in.
- How it was found – e.g. by trowelling or screening.

Field forms are used to provide an in-depth description of each excavation level and on field inventory forms you list bags of finds as they are recovered. This list then becomes the field specimen catalogue, with each bag being assigned a field catalogue number which is written on the bags and form. A simple numbering system would be to use the site number followed by sequential numbers for each bag.

Other forms are used to record information about a variety of things such as individual features and the stratigraphy of an excavated unit's wall.

A digger's official field notes will include even more in-depth information than the various forms. You should keep a written record of *everything* you do in a single day that might impact on how your data and findings are interpreted – such as the weather conditions, any issues with equipment, and what finds, units, strata or levels you worked on.

Hand-held computers are being increasingly used to record information about the context of finds, but paper records should also be kept as a backup.

Section Drawings

Once a feature has been fully excavated, the archaeologist draws and photographs their vertical sections. This serves as a permanent record of the original condition of the site, as well as revealing how it fits in with other archaeological deposits. Because the section drawing cuts all the way through the feature, you can get a good idea of its story.

Before you can start drawing, use your trowel to make the vertical face as straight as possible. A datum (or base) line is then established to take measurements from, and – at the top of the section – a piece of string is stretched from one side to the other (using a small spirit level to ensure it is horizontal).

Once you've done this, you can run a tape measure along the string to serve as the drawing's horizontal scale. A second hand-held tape measure can then be used to take vertical readings from the string.

You are now ready to begin your section drawing.

Use one of the thicker lines on the graph paper to represent the string, with arrows on either side. The sides of the ditch are then measured and drawn in relation to the datum line. To do this, transfer your measurements onto tracing paper in the form of dots before joining them together to reflect the outline of the ditch.

The next stage involves drawing the horizons of the layers that fill the ditch, as well as large objects (such as stones) in the ditch fill.

Last of all, the section drawing is labelled with the scale, the orientation, the context numbers of layers and features, the site and trench numbers, the date the drawing was produced, and the digger's initials.

Photographs

A photographic record *must* be kept at every stage of a site's excavation. Photographs have a range of uses – from being an integral part of the site record, to placing features or even the site in their wider context, to serving as an additional check against drawings and context sheets. For educational purposes, it is also a good idea to take more general pictures of diggers at work during the excavation.

When taking photographs, you might want to spray the area with water to enhance the contrast in soil colours. Most importantly though, make sure everything is evenly lit and that photos of archaeological deposits prior to being removed contain a scale and an arrow pointing north. Because the area being photographed needs to be clean and free of debris, tools, string, nails and other irrelevant material, photography is left until last.

Processing Finds in a Laboratory

Archaeological laboratories can be found in a range of institutions: namely universities, museums and offices of certain government agencies.

Sometimes field labs are set up on archaeological sites so excavated finds can be attended to straight away. The basic process of taking care of finds involves:

- Cleaning and repairing them.
- Storing them in a rational easy-to-find manner and in appropriate conditions.

Some key characteristics of an ideal lab are:

- Clean and well lit.
- Sufficient space for both work and storage.
- Climate-controlled and pollution-free to prevent finds from deteriorating.
- Secure

Labs also require a range of fittings and supplies. Some examples are:

- High-intensity lamps.
- Tables and chairs.
- Adjustable shelving.
- A map cabinet with large drawers.
- A large sink (including a sand trap that deposits soil in a container to prevent clogging up the pipes).
- Screens with varying mesh sizes to search soil samples.
- Computers, printers, scanners and software for processing data, creating maps, etc.

- Common lab items, such as scales, magnets, microscopes, beakers and pipettes.
- Plastic tubs (used for washing finds in).
- Waterproof pens and quill pens with black and white India (indelible) ink.
- Measuring equipment, including rulers, protractors, compasses and calipers.
- Acid-free paper bags and resealable plastic bags (of varying sizes).
- Sturdy boxes and padding for storing finds.
- Small excavation tools such as butter knives and dental picks for chipping dirt off finds.
- Acryloid B-72 solution, polyvinyl acetate, acetone, Duco cement, white glue and clear nail polish for preservation work. Use a container with clean sand to hold artefacts that have been glued back together while they dry.
- Refrigerator (for storing film and fragile finds).

Processing finds

Archaeological finds should be cleaned, stabilised or repaired (if needed), identified, classified and catalogued, and measured and photographed before being put into storage. In the ideal lab all these things will be done at the same time to restrict the amount of times artefacts are taken out of their bags and potentially damaged, but in the majority of labs there is not the space or labour to do this.

Washing finds

Attempting to clean finds in a sink risks clogging the drain, so use toothbrushes and tubs filled with water instead (which can be emptied outside once you're finished).

Some techniques to remember when washing archaeological remains include:

- Never separate a find from its provenience during the washing and drying process.

- Don't wash finds that look fragile.
- Don't wash finds that contain deposits that might provide valuable information (such as blood).
- Finds made from hard materials such as stone should be brushed gently and kept underwater to avoid splashing muddy water across the lab.
- Unglazed prehistoric ceramics can sometimes be cleaned very easily – by immersing them in water and gently rubbing the find with your fingertips.
- Organic finds (such as wood, cloth, feathers and bone) should be rinsed or dry-brushed and – depending on the item – may need immediate conservation measures to be taken such as keeping them wet or soaking them in preservative solutions.

- Only brush shells and hard bone when absolutely necessary (using a soft brush).
- Softer bones might be too fragile to clean. If they aren't, rinse or dry-brush them.
- Be careful when chipping rust off iron artefacts as they may be fragile or rusted all the way through. Use metal tools to do this.

Conserving or restoring finds

While *conserving* finds refers to taking measures to prevent archaeological material from deteriorating, *restoring* them takes it a step further by attempting to return them to their original condition.

Conservation: *Anything* recovered from salt water needs to be soaked to remove the salt, and preservative solutions can be used to prevent crumbling bone or potsherds deteriorating further.

Acryloid B-72 and polyvinyl acetate (PVA) are two commonly used chemicals to stabilise archaeological material, although white glue (containing PVA), a thin solution of Duco cement or acetone (nail polish remover minus the oils and scents) can do the job too. The drawbacks of using such chemicals include jeopardising any chance of radiocarbon dating the find or of conducting bone mineral analysis.

To prevent rusted metal finds from rusting even more, place them in an *electrolysis bath* (if a sufficient amount of the object is still intact) to draw the corrosion out. Similarly, wooden finds recovered from waterlogged sites can be soaked in warm polyethylene glycol (PEG) which gradually replaces the water in the object. In both cases, they often have to remain submerged in these baths for months on end, meaning valuable laboratory space is taken up.

On a more optimistic note, hard materials such as stone and ceramics do not normally require any conservation.

To restore or not to restore? Reconstructing artefacts (reassembling them and filling in any gaps using modern materials) can be a useful way of interpreting the past, and they look great in exhibits. However, if you want to study the find further in the future it is better to preserve the object with minimal treatment rather than restore it.

Soil samples

Bags of soil samples taken from the site can now be searched for small fragments of archaeological material using flotation – pouring the soil through water and fine mesh screens. As explained in the previous chapter, larger objects will appear in the *heavy fraction* (the largest screen) and smaller objects will appear in the *light fraction* (the smallest screen).

Once the flotation process is complete and the material recovered has been left to dry out, they need to be sorted into categories. The dried remains are poured onto a tray and sorted through with instruments such as tweezers or wooden sticks, before being sorted into bags or vials based on their type (e.g. stone, shell or seed). Due to the size of some of the material recovered, this will require a magnifying glass – and don't forget to label each bag or container with its provenience!

Some small soil samples, meanwhile, might be spared the flotation process, dried out (to prevent mould growth) and put in boxes for further study.

Cataloguing

Once all the finds have been cleaned, they must be numbered and catalogued to prevent their provenience being lost. Cataloguing involves a number of tasks, including:

- Updating the field catalogue with new information found in the lab.
- Producing individual catalogue sheets for each bag from each provenience. Now they're clean enough to establish what the items are, list all the materials contained in each bag, as well as attributes such as their weight and dimensions.
- Assign each find a catalogue number and write it on the find. These will vary depending on what system you use. In some cases you might keep the catalogue numbers used during the excavation (e.g. the site number followed by a sequential number for each find). Some institutions (such as museums), however, label all their artefacts with long accession numbers which are then stored on a large database.

Catalogue numbers should always be written on the finds themselves, and can be done using the following guidelines:

- As a standard, use quill pens with metal tips (to prevent hard materials wearing them out) and black India (indelible) ink.
- Use white India (indelible) ink for writing on dark-coloured finds (but make sure you use a separate pen so your ink colours don't mix).
- In some cases (such as with porous materials) clear nail polish is needed to create a small solid surface to write on. Do not attempt to write the number until the polish has dried completely.
- If finds cannot be written on (such as rusty iron objects) write the number on a paper tag and tie it to the object with string.
- Try to write the number on parts of the find that are unlikely to be photographed and do not contain significant features.

Artefact classification

Once the artefacts have been cleaned and assigned a catalogue number, lay them out to see what you have. You should then be able to give the items a general identification – maybe based on artefact type or raw material – before moving on to use *artefact typologies*. Artefact typologies are guides listing the types of artefacts associated with a specific geographical area. The best typologies have criteria that do not overlap, allowing finds to be sorted into clear categories, although a great many are not this sophisticated. It is often necessary to describe the item and note down the artefact type it most closely resembles, or even to establish a new artefact type.

Here are some pointers for identifying and sorting your finds:

- Some pottery is easy to classify by observing its decoration and whether it was painted on or moulded into the clay while it was still wet. Names attributed to ceramic types are normally based on their appearance or the place where they were first found.

- Chipped stone tools can be divided into *unifacial* (flaked on one side) and *bifacial* (flaked on both sides). Each of these can be subdivided into other artefact types.
- *Lithic debitage* is the term used for flakes and other debris produced from chipping stone tools. Two main types include *primary flakes* (which still contain some of the outer stone) and *secondary flakes* (the inner material, which is normally flatter and of better quality), and these can be subdivided further based on factors such as size, colour and type of stone.
- Stone artefacts that were formed by smoothing or grinding rather than chipping are known as *ground-stone* artefacts, and can range from bowls to axes to statues.
- Some organic artefacts (made of materials such as bone, shell or wood) that have deteriorated too much to identify might have to be broadly classified as worked fragments.
- Metal artefacts are initially classified by their raw material, before being subdivided into more complex categories that can be determined with the help of expert advice or guidebooks detailing typical types of finds in the region of concern.
- Historic items and materials such as glass, earthenware (softer), stoneware (harder) and china are described and classified in a range of guidebooks. In the case of glass, it can be subdivided based on its colour, shape, and whether it is hand-blown (less symmetrical) or produced by machine (featuring mould marks).

- *Granulometric analysis* is the term used for classifying soil types by their grain size – sand (large, medium and small), silt and clay.
- Biological specimens are normally comparatively easier to identify than archaeological remains. Use guidebooks on the skeletons or shells of various species to help you find a precise classification.

Paperwork

The report for your archaeological investigation should always contain a well-drafted map(s) that is fit for publication. This could be a large map of the entire site, maps focusing on each unit and their features in detail or three-dimensional images of each unit's strata and contents.

Some other paper records from the excavation you might need to put into digital format include:

- Field forms
- Photo logs
- Notes of fellow participants.
- Drawings of features.
- Drawings of a unit's floor and wall stratigraphy.
- Historic or environmental records relevant to the site.
- Catalogues and data from previous investigations conducted at the same site.

Curation and Collections Management

The word *curation* refers to storing archaeological materials and records as well as ensuring they are available for use in future investigations.

The term *collections management*, meanwhile, is also used to refer to facilitating further research with archaeological materials and records.

Some museums have dedicated areas for visiting researchers, and laboratories should always have a few empty tables reserved in case someone wants to study some of the archaeological material stored there. Labs and museums with larger budgets and workforces might even have all their collections catalogued online for researchers to access.

Accessibility is important seeing as excavating archaeological remains and then failing to process, study and look after the data and materials obtained is unethical and amounts to looting. If artefacts are well looked after new techniques or technology might be able to obtain new information from finds in the future, and therefore effective collections management is just as important in archaeological research as the excavation process.

Analysing Archaeological Finds

Charting finds

Artefact tables are a useful way of presenting what you've dug up in a logical fashion. They take many forms and can be created using a spreadsheet – allowing you to easily extract the information you're looking for from a pile of data by sorting by column or row.

Charting finds in horizontal space: In order to work out the differences between separate horizontal sections of a site a list needs to be produced – showing how many of each artefact type were found and where.

Charting finds in vertical space: The distribution of artefacts in vertical space in each unit can reveal how activities and styles have changed over time. Types of finds are inserted into a table based on their level or strata (with artefacts from disturbed areas such as the ground surface being excluded).

Converting your tables: Information from artefact tables can be presented quickly and effectively with charts and graphs, and can reveal all sorts of patterns, such as the increase or decrease in popularity of certain artefact types and styles over time. The organisation of data into tables, charts and graphs, therefore, can give a much clearer picture of changes that occurred at the site over time and lead to findings that are just as eye-catching as anything you might find during an excavation.

Mapping finds: Maps are essential for identifying patterns at archaeological sites. During fieldwork a map will already have been produced detailing the locations of geographical features and excavation units, and now it is time to add any information extracted from clusters of artefacts and ecofacts. These distribution maps can be drawn by hand or produced using computer graphics programs.

Some of the things the finished maps might reveal is the clustering of certain artefact, feature or soil types in certain areas, a connection between one artefact type and another, and any unexcavated areas close to the most significant finds that may require further investigation.

Analysing materials

After sorting your finds into different classifications or types, further analysis is still required.

Basic analyses: Significant attributes such as the shape, style or decoration of a find can be used to further distinguish them from each other, leading to more data and tables being produced.

Use-wear analysis: This involves searching artefacts for signs of how they were changed or damaged as a result of use (known as *use-wear*) and from this identifying their function. Such analyses are particularly common with stone tools, where their sharp edges are dulled by cutting or scraping.

Artefact composition: It is sometimes possible to analyse the different raw materials artefacts are composed of by merely looking at them. The raw material can be added to artefact tables to reveal a range of interesting information, such as how far away past people were from the resources they used. Objects made from materials from further afield might indicate the item's greater value as well as interaction taking place with non-local peoples.

Dating

While *direct dating* methods date the artefact itself, *indirect dating* methods date the age of something the artefact is associated with.

For example, due to the absence of carbon in stone, radiocarbon dating cannot be used to date it. However, you can estimate the age of stone artefacts based on their appearance or style, where they're found and what they're found with.

Relative dating methods, on the other hand, provide an artefact's age in relation to something else rather than an actual date. Some examples include:

- **The law of superposition:** assumes artefacts buried deeper in the ground are older than those buried closer to the surface (provided the soil hasn't been churned up).
- **Seriation:** is where artefacts are arranged based on similarities in style or the frequency of their occurrence (with those that look most alike being placed closest to each other on the chart). This works with any artefacts that change over time, although its principal pitfall is that many artefacts do not change gradually over time.
- **Fluorine dating:** can be used to determine the amount of time an object has been underground. This method assumes that items that can absorb fluorine in the soil (such as bones) will take up the same amount if they are buried in the same place at the same time, and from this can be confirmed as being the same age.

Two ways of obtaining a precise date in years for an artefact is by using *absolute* or *chronometric dating*. Absolute dating can only be used on objects such as coins (which have the date written on them). Chronometric dating, meanwhile, measures the amount of time that has passed, with its most well-known method being radiocarbon dating. Radiocarbon dating can determine the age of an object containing organic material by analysing the radioactive decay of the carbon-14 isotope. When any living organism dies the carbon-14 it took in in life through eating (and other means) starts to decay at a known rate (measured by the *half-life* – how long it takes half of it to decay). The half-life of carbon-14 is 5,730 years, and this can be used to calculate how much time has passed since the organism died.

Although radiocarbon dating is an incredibly useful dating method, it does have its drawbacks:

- The material needs to be organic and preserved in a sufficient quantity.
- Radiocarbon dating isn't accurate 100% of the time, and may sometimes give you an incorrect date.
- It cannot be used to date organisms much older than 50,000 years (because of the half-life), so cannot be applied to much of humanity's two-million-year-long existence.

Another well-known chronometric dating method is *dendrochronology* (tree-dating). This involves examining tree rings to determine when they first started to grow. The characteristics of the rings depend on the weather conditions the tree grew in, and therefore the method works best in areas with high variability such as deserts. It also requires the artefact to have enough wood to see the rings (and for the archaeologist to be aware that the wood might have already been old when it was used to make the artefact).

As well as dating artefacts, dendrochronology can also be used to calibrate radiocarbon dates to ensure they are accurate.

Reconstructing the Human Past

Archaeologists seek to study the workings of past human cultures, as well as how they changed and adapted, where they succeeded and failed, and how they rose and fell.

In addition to this an archaeological study can be *synchronic* (explaining what happened at a specific time in the site's history) or *diachronic* (revealing how the site – or perhaps even the entire region – changed over time).

Amongst the easiest past human activities to reconstruct are subsistence (people's livelihoods), technology (what resources people had and how they obtained them) and dating (how long ago).

Determining how social and political systems operated and what people believed (their *ideology*), on the other hand, is often a lot harder to understand from archaeological evidence alone.

Because of the ambiguity that frequently plagues archaeological work, when interpreting your finds in the project report start with the safe suggestions about them first before moving on to present more speculative ideas.

Interpreting daily life

Artefacts, ecofacts, features and soil can yield a wealth of information about the mundane elements of past peoples' lives, while environmental data, site distribution maps and *artefact sourcing* (finding out the origin of artefacts) can reveal where people settled and how people and goods were moved.

Environment: Finding archaeological evidence concerning the impact of the environment on past peoples and how they shaped it, adapted to it or were otherwise affected by it can be of great value in the present day. In order to illustrate how past peoples' natural surroundings shaped their way of life (*cultural ecology*), you must establish what resources would have been available to people living on the site at a given time (the ecological setting), as well as the locations of other sites and what other societies existed at the same time (to establish the environmental setting as fully as possible). As well as seeking to find out how people dealt with environmental change, you can also find evidence for how they manipulated the environment to their advantage (for example, through domestication or the construction of canals and irrigation channels).

Subsistence: A great deal of information about how people acquired food and other resources can be revealed by artefacts and features, such as tools used for hunting or agriculture. In addition to this ecofacts can be used to tell you some of the species of animals and plants past people used and in what quantity. However, as a note of caution, you must be aware that they might have had a different use rather than food (e.g. for making tools), and that they might not represent their entire diet (some remains might have been discarded elsewhere) or all the wildlife present in the past environment (many animals and plants might not have been used by people).

Technology: In many ways it is easy to establish what technology was used at a site in the past by examining artefacts and structural remains for clues regarding their use and how they were made. However, this may be easier said than done if the items were not used for routine everyday purposes or if vital parts of them (usually organic) have rotted away.

Economics: By comparing what was available at a site and the surrounding region and what wasn't, you can begin to reconstruct the economic systems of past people by determining what goods they were trading and what they were getting in return. In addition to this, by studying the distribution of specific artefacts and resources across the site you can begin to see how egalitarian past societies were (whether wealth was concentrated in the hands of a few privileged individuals or shared amongst the masses).

Settlement systems

The relationship between different sites at different times within a given region is known as the *inter-site settlement system*, and can reveal a range of patterns. For example, one type of site might be typically found in different locations to another type of site – with economic centres being based near waterways to facilitate the transportation of goods and people, and religious shrines being found in more isolated 'holy' places such as mountains. The location of sites might also have moved as peoples' cultures and ways of life changed – with hunter-gatherers favouring more rugged or forested terrain, before shifting to more fertile land when they adopted settled agriculture.

Social systems

A social system can be classified in terms of its size, success, and division of wealth and labour, amongst other things. Other categories are based on the complexity of the society, with some examples of these classifications being:

- *Egalitarian societies*: lack social stratification, and are characterised by a relatively equal distribution of wealth and people performing similar occupations. People normally acquire food by simple means (such as by foraging) and move from site to site depending on the time of year to acquire different resources when they're in season. A division of labour might exist based on age or gender, but groups tend to be small seeing as more complicated social organisation is required for larger numbers of people. Archaeological remains of egalitarian societies, therefore, tend to be found on small sites with noticeable similarities between the occupants – such as in housing, health and forms of burial.

- *Ranked societies*: associate rank with power and ascribe social positions to individuals based on their genealogical distance from the chief. Some members of these societies might specialise in occupations unrelated to farming and obtain their food through the labour of others. Subsistence is typically based on a mixture of foraging, hunting and agriculture and, even though different people have different titles and social positions, they still use and share the same resources. Archaeological remains of a ranked society can be detected by the presence of high-status graves or rich artefacts in a select few houses but with no significant difference between the wealth and health of the inhabitants.

- *Stratified societies*: are partly organised around formal social stratification (such as caste, class or estate) and restrict access to resources and rank to some people. There is real wealth inequality between individuals and their leaders have the power to make and enforce rules. In most societies the emergence of social stratification arises alongside an intensification in agriculture – with ambitious projects such as the construction of roads and irrigation systems being made much easier using slave labour. In comparison to egalitarian and ranked societies, archaeological signs of stratified societies are much easier to identify – marked by different housing, concentrations of rich artefacts, and human remains reflecting a division of wealth and labour (with some showing signs of hard labour, and others being better fed and in good health).

- *State-level societies*: are the most complex in terms of social, economic and political organization, and have a formal government and clearly defined social classes. States control or influence many areas of its members' lives, and can punish dissidents, levy taxes and establish large cities, amongst other things. They are made possible by large-scale agriculture and the domestication of animals, allowing the majority of the labour force to be moved into occupations outside food production. Their large settlements, sophistication and unequal wealth distribution are easy to detect in the archaeological record.

It is often the case that no broad category sufficiently describes the social organisation of a culture, making it necessary to combine bits from different classifications.

Kinship: Many past societies were organised in terms of one's *kin* or family, with a range of things in the archaeological record reflecting family affiliation such as symbols or a cluster of houses.

Ethnicity: This was another way of broadly organising past societies, although ethnic identities are often surprisingly hard to find using archaeological evidence. Even though bone and tooth analysis can sometimes be used to determine if a person was native to the area where their remains were found, ethnic identity is just as much determined by who you associate yourself with socially and culturally as it is by biology. Nor are artefacts often of much use. Many belongings in your home do not reflect your nationality, and just because you own items associated with a particular place (such as Coca-Cola) it does not mean you identify yourself with that social group (Americans).

Gender: Differences vary from extreme to minimal depending on the culture, and it is often very tricky to find solid archaeological evidence for gender divisions in past societies. When interpreting any findings, it is important not to impose the models of your own society on past cultures – something that might be made easier by comparing the organisation of other known societies that existed at the same time as the one you're studying. Burials are one way of finding out some information (because you can tell the gender), but even then it is not easy to interpret the evidence seeing as it is often impossible to tell what the symbols or items they were buried with meant by the standards of the past society.

Politics: This exists in all societies, although its form and complexity can vary dramatically. Labour, decision-making and the enforcement of those decisions is normally a communal effort in simpler societies, whereas more complex societies feature individuals or groups with more power than others. Some sure signs of more complicated political systems include human sacrifice (where an individual or group has the power of life and death over others) and organised warfare (where an individual or group has the means of mobilising vast amounts of people and resources).

Archaeological Reports

All archaeologists have an ethical obligation to produce a report of their findings – failure to do so will result in them being no better than looters.

Archaeological reports describe all the work you carried out on a project, including research, fieldwork and lab work. They also detail your findings, what they reveal about past human behaviour, and what additional research is required in the future. Ideally, the publication will be thorough enough to allow other archaeologists to look at the data and agree, disagree, or take the interpretation further – or in a different direction.

Reports should contain sections containing the following information:

- Introduction explaining why you chose to do the project and what its goals were, as well as a list of crew members and any sources of support.
- The site's environmental background (e.g. what resources were available to past people there).
- The site's cultural background (what past peoples are known to have been active there).
- The site's archaeological background (what archaeologists have found there in the past and how this relates to their project).
- Fieldwork – including background research, where you excavated, how deep you dug, what methods you used, and your reasoning for these decisions.
- Lists of all the soils, strata and features excavated during the project, and an explanation of what information they yield.
- Lists of all the material uncovered during the project (often ordered by their type), and a discussion of what

the *assemblage* (entire group) of each kind can tell us.

- What your project's findings indicate about past human activity and in what ways it met or didn't meet your initial research goals.
- Illustrations and photographs of the site's landscape, the excavation or any significant finds.
- Maps of the site and a discussion of how the site relates to other archaeological sites in the area.
- Suggestions for any future work that could be carried out at the site, and information about where future researchers can access your finds and data.
- If the project was carried out for the purpose of cultural resources management (CRM) you will also need to make suggestions regarding if the site is expendable and the development can go ahead as planned or if there is significant archaeology at the site that requires further study or even protecting from the development.

The finished report is normally submitted to whoever funded the work. Copies should also be sent to:

- Everyone who worked on the project.
- The landowner and any other interested individuals.
- Anyone who provided you with information during the project.

- The government agency that granted you permission to investigate the site.
- Local and university libraries.

Today an increasing number of archaeological reports are being made available online, although this is not always a good idea seeing as it gives looters greater information about the location of archaeological sites.

What certainly is good practice, however, is to write an article for publication in an academic journal about your project to make your results available to fellow researchers.

Thinking ahead

Unfortunately archaeological investigations rarely answer all the questions the archaeologists sought to answer at the start of the project, and many new questions are raised during the investigation. But that does not make it a fruitless exercise. Piece by piece, with new studies and the assistance of new technology, our understanding of individual sites – and in turn human history as a whole – is growing.

After a project is completed, then, it is the job of future researchers to pick up from where they left off and pursue these new lines of enquiry.

Printed in Dunstable, United Kingdom